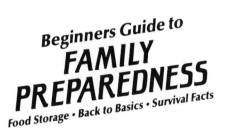

Beginners Guide to
FAMILY
PREPAREDNESS
Food Storage • Back to Basics • Survival Facts

Beginners Guide to
FAMILY
PREPAREDNESS
Food Storage • Back to Basics • Survival Facts

Rosalie Mason

Seventh Printing: March 1999

International Standard Book Number
0-88290-082-X

Horizon Publishers' Catalog and Order Number
1217

Printed and distributed
in the United States of America by

& Distributors, Incorporated

Mailing Address:
P.O. Box 490
Bountiful, Utah 84011-0490

Street Address:
50 South 500 West
Bountiful, Utah 84010

Phone and Fax:
Local Phone: (801) 295-9451
WATS (toll free): 1 (800) 453-0812
FAX: (801) 295-0196

Internet:
E-mail: horizonp@burgoyne.com
Home Page: http:// www.horizonpublishers.com

This book is dedicated with love

to my children

Wayne

Johnny

Debbie

Tommy

Paul

Priscilla

and

Marshal

for all the happiness they have given me,

and to my

seventeen grandchildren.

They are my pride and joy.

Acknowledgments

I would like to acknowledge with grateful appreciation the guidance and support while I was engaged in writing the original manuscript of my friend, Rendal V. Broomhead. His help was greatly appreciated. My gratitude is also extended to my close friend, Larry Quinn, for his editing, critical reviews, and helpful suggestions.

Thanks to my dear friend, Ruth Potter, for her faith, encouragement, and prayers, and most of all for her professional help in compiling the medical chapter.

Many thanks, also, to Charlene Earwood, Maxine Cutler, Mary Marshal, and Jane and Stanley Latimer for the hours spent typing the rough manuscript.

To my son, Marshal, for his cooperation in taking over my household responsibilities while I was writing this book, and to my son Wayne for his long hours spent designing the beautiful cover and illustrations contained in this work, I want to express my undying love and gratitude.

My appreciation is also extended to Floyd and Joanne Jensen for their technical advice in preparing the original manuscript.

I would also like to give very special thanks to my husband John. He has the wisdom of Solomon. He is my strength and inspiration, and his collaboration made this volume possible.

And most of all, I humbly express my deep gratitude to my Heavenly Father for all he so abundantly gives.

Preface

The aim of this book is to present the basic facts and techniques of a home storage and production program in as simple and interesting a manner as possible, and to teach how such knowledge may be utilized to the fullest extent. With each revision we have endeavored to teach the economy of a year's supply of food reserves and non-food necessities, and to stress the value of the peace of mind which comes from knowing your family will be fed and clothed should a time of difficulty arise.

With the drought situation as it stands today, and the mountain snow pack far below normal, many of our western states are considered disaster areas. In view of this, governments may be compelled to force curtailment of both water and power. We may be in the unique situation of having our modern conveniences stand idle while we learn the skills our fathers used many years ago, such as: sun dehydrating, home canning, curing meat to preserve our food, cooking on a wood stove to feed our children, and washing our clothes on a rub board in order to have clean clothing.

It is also the aim of this book to develop a guide to provide people with written instructions to teach them the "do's," "don'ts," and "how to's" of a successful home storage program. Therein lies the reason for this publication.

The Beginners Guide to Family Preparedness is designed to answer basic questions and to give sound advice in many facets of home storage and production.

Rosalie Mason

About the Author
Rosalie Mason

During her childhood, Rosalie Mason was involved in several experiences which taught her the importance of personal and family preparedness. She was born during the great depression. While she was still a young child, their family lost the grocery store they operated in Oklahoma. Lack of income made it necessary for the children to be divided among relatives in order to survive.

When the family was reunited, they made their way to San Bernardino, California in 1937. They were living in a motel near a river when heavy rains burst the dam above them. They fled for high ground, barely escaping with their lives, but witnessed the pandemonium of a severe flood that took hundreds of lives.

Rosalie graduated from high school in Chula Vista, married John Mason, and attended Southwestern College there, but had to withdraw when their five children were stricken with scarlet fever.

These and other experiences taught her the importance of being self-sufficient. Through most of her life she has raised her own garden, and has been engaged in food storage activities, quilting, making bread and soap, canning and drying food, etc.

The family moved to Everett, Washington in 1966 and then to Longview, Washington in 1975. In Washington she began demonstrating the preparedness techniques she had learned to clubs and church groups. She is working towards a degree in Nutrition from the Brigham Young University.

Rosalie is a convert to The Church of Jesus Christ of Latter-day Saints, and has served in presidencies of the MIA, Primary, and Relief Society, as well as teaching classes in the various church auxiliaries. The first edition of this book was written when she and her husband were asked by local church leaders to serve as "Stake Home Production and Storage Specialists" and to write an instruction booklet on food storage and family preparedness for church members in her area.

Table of Contents

Part Five
Survival Mechanics

Part Six
Diversified Food Preparation

Part Seven
Tips on Techniques

Part Eight
Survival Library

Part 1

Answers to Four Simple Questions

Chapter One

Why Should We Store?

In recent years we have heard much from civil authorities concerning the storage of food in case of an emergency, their thinking being influenced primarily by premonitions of famine, warfare, or civil strife. We are concerned about the welfare of our people in times of sickness, accident, unemployment or other incidents that might suspend income or availability of supplies.

Before our national economy made it convenient for us to get what we wanted by merely having the purchase price, man was in the habit of providing enough of the necessities of life for himself and family to last from one harvest to the next. People in those days were careful to plan ahead for future needs. We believe their custom of being prepared was a wise one, and people would do well to continue the preparedness practice today.

People Lived from Harvest to Harvest

Many years ago our grandfathers used to fill their pantries from harvest to harvest, going into town to purchase needed supplies only three or four times a year.

In the fall cattle, hogs and sheep were butchered, brine cured, and set aside in the cellar for winter food. Garden vegetables were canned, root vegetables were buried in the root cellar, leek, onions and garlic were hung on strong twine from the ceiling in the cellar to dry. Berries were gathered with other fruit, and jam and jellies were made and stored in the cellar with the other winter food. Corn was gathered, shucked, dried, and taken to a neighbor's grist mill to be ground into the winter supply of cornmeal. The meal was poured into barrels and it too, was stored in the cellar.

Sugar cane was cut, the juice extracted, and grandfather would fire up the syrup cooker where the juice would be painstakenly cooked until syrup was made. The pure ribbon cane syrup was poured into gallon buckets, labeled and stored away with the rest of the year's harvest. Neighbors from near and far would bring their cane to grandfather to be made into syrup.

After all the vegetables were harvested, syrup made, and meat was in the brine, a list of staples would be compiled to round out the winter food needs. Since the family traveled by wagon and it was the only way of transporting supplies, trips into town were made only three or four times a year; yet our grandfathers were prepared for any eventuality.

Bread Winner Injured in Industrial Accident

In our travels we have come into contact with people who live from pay check to pay check and have no food reserves put aside, and these same people have had a variety of incidents suspend their income for prolonged periods of time.

A few years ago a family was called to our attention by a mutual friend. The father was involved in an industrial accident in which both his feet were broken. He was kept in the hospital overnight, and then returned home to face the dilemma of being confined to a wheelchair for nine long months with no income other than a small state compensation insurance check. If he and his wife had counseled together with foresight, and systematically accumulated a year's food reserves, how much easier this tragedy could have been. While we enjoy the convenience of the corner grocery store, we should not lose sight of the ever-present possibility that a time may come when our income stops and we will not be able to purchase the goods we need, or worse still, that though we may have the purchasing power we might not have food or commodities available.

Family of Five Lives Nearly Two Years on Food Reserves

There is another family we would like to mention. Like the other family, the father was in an industrial accident. His leg was severely broken in four places between the knee and ankle. Father Smith, like Father Brown, received state compensation insurance. He also had to face the realization that he would be unable to work for at least a year-and-a-half. It has been nearly two years since the accident, yet Father Smith was so prepared with a year's food reserves and other necessities, he has not shifted from himself the responsibility of taking care of his family.

We have observed that most people never consider that they might find themselves in a disaster situation—they somehow think it always happens to the "other fellow."

"The Big Drought of 1975"

In 1954, the late I.R. Tannehill, who was then chief of the U.S. Weather Bureau (now the Weather Service), warned in the middle of the previous U.S. drought cycle: "What will we do when the great drought of 1975 settles down upon us?" Tannehill, at that time, accurately foretold the good years we have since experienced as well as pinpointing the floods which ravaged widespread parts of America in the 1970's. (Mr. Tannehill's forecasts were made in the September 1954 issue of Country Gentlemen magazine.)

Matthew 24:7—A Prophetic Warning

One of the most emphatic prophetic signs foreshadowing the end of this age of man and the establishment of the long-overlooked world-ruling kingdom of God was that there would be "famines, and pestilences, and earthquakes, in divers places." (Matthew 24:7). Who knows how long it will be till these events influence us on a personal basis?

The United States—The Land of Milk and Honey

With this prediction in mind let us explore, then, the possibility of a famine. The United States has always been referred to as the "land of milk and honey", or the "land of plenty". We have experienced many years of good, abundant crops. With food everywhere, many of us have never felt the gnawing pangs of hunger.

The drought of 1975 is behind us—so is the critical winter of 1976 with less snow pack and rain in the west than ever before. The winter wheat crop had to be ploughed under and replanted. The severe cold in Florida ruined the 1977 summer citrus fruit and tomato crop, therefore it would seem the predictions found in Matthew and reinterated by the late Mr. Tannehill, by scientific means seems to be occurring.

Individual Family Food Reserves Help Feed
Teton Dam Disaster Victims

The cities involved in the flood caused by the Teton dam disaster had been taught by their church to store a year's supply of food, bedding, medical supplies, emergency cooking fuel, a two week supply of water, vitamin C, and where possible, material and clothing. These generous people were able to provide necessary food and blankets for families who had lost everything until the Red Cross and federal government were able to ship truck loads of aid to the unfortunate victims.

The information we have given we believe to be true, sound and factual. We have tried to give evidence that the living from pay check to pay check concept does not give adequate protection to a family in the event an emergency situation should arise.

Food Reserves More Essential Than Money Reserves

We urge you to reasses your position concerning a practical storage program for your particular family.

We feel food reserves are more essential than money reserves. There may be a time when you have suitcases filled with money and yet not have enough to buy a loaf of bread or a quart of milk.

This happened in Germany between 1915 and 1924. A customer came into my store in California requesting information on food storage. After chatting a few minutes, she informed me she was, in fact, in Germany during this period of time. This sweet lady, with tears in her eyes, stated her grandchildren were going to have the food she could not purchase for her own children. The lady worked as an accountant in Germany, and her last pay check was six billion dollars. She actually carried the money in two suitcases and could not purchase the needed food for her daughter. Finally, relatives who were living here in the United States sent steamship tickets for her family to move to New York.

Illness Ravages Village—No Food or Soap

Another customer—I'll call him Mr. Chex—came into my store with his lovely wife to inquire about storing food. Mr. Chex was in Czechoslovakia during World War II. The village he lived in had no food and, what was just as bad, no soap. Mr. Chex remembers vividly the hunger in the village, he and the other children ate grass and were very glad to get it. He remembers too, the infection and illness that was prevalent because they had no soap to wash their bodies, clothes or homes.

We could go on endlessly with one case history after another. However, our position is not to use scare tactics, but rather to inform and say, "Don't Panic!" Sit down as a family and make a plan for your family that is suitable both financially and practically. There are few families who have the financial resources to purchase randomly, therefore there may be sacrifices you as a family will have to make. We urge you to make them and put away the food reserves to sustain your family for at least a year.

Chapter Two

What Should We Store?

The question most often asked is, "What Should We Store?"

Too often the inexperienced tend to relate a year's supply to their weekly food purchases in cost and storage space. They think of the many items they must buy on a weekly basis to satisfy the need of their family. They ponder the cost of these items, multiply by fifty-two weeks and the end results are astronomical! They are *defeated* before they begin the *storage program*.

A suggestion made by an individual who was intensely interested in food storage may be the solution to the dilemma. The man was Harold B. Lee, who spoke at the meeting on welfare on October 1, 1966:

Perhaps if we think not in terms of a year's supply of what we ordinarily would use and think more in terms of what it would take to keep us alive in case we didn't have anything else to eat, that would be very easy to put in storage for a year,...and if you think in terms of that kind of annual storage rather than a whole year's supply of everything that you are accustomed to eating, which, in most cases, is utterly impossible for the average family, I think we will come nearer to what President Clark advised us way back in 1937.

Home Storage should begin with basic items that will sustain life in an emergency. Later, after these have been obtained in adequate amounts, consideration could be given to storing foods that are ordinarily eaten. The choice of which foods to store must be based on a consideration of food value and storage qualities.

Carbohydrates, fats, proteins, vitamins, and minerals are essential for good health. Many foods that are adaptable for long storage either lack certain essential vitamins or lose vitamins during storage. When only basic foods are stored, therefore, they need to be supplemented with foods that will supply adequate amounts of vitamin C and A (Fruits and vegetables).

Beginning. One-Month Storage Program

The following list of items are for an emergency storage for a family of four for one month. The Red Cross, Nutritionists, and doctors agree that the minimum caloric requirement for adults is around 1858 calories per day. Taken in proper amounts, powdered milk, wheat products, peanuts or peanut butter, and tomato juice will supply the basic needs for all adults except the extreme cases. Following are the proper proportions for the above mentioned foods for each day's consumption:

Daily Adult Proportions for Emergency Storage for a Family of Four for One Month

Four (4) 8 oz. glasses of powered milk	980 Calories
Three (3) oz. shredded wheat, wheat germ, or whole wheat	318 Calories
Four (4) oz. peanuts or	420 Calories
One Tablespoon peanut butter	95 Calories
Eight (8) oz. tomato juice	45 Calories
Total	1858 Calories

The preceding items have been tabulated and an estimated cost is shown below for a family of four for one month.

35 lbs. powdered milk	$35.00
22 lbs. whole wheat	3.08
34 lbs. raw peanuts	18.70
30-30 oz. cans tomato juice	19.50
Total Estimate Cost	$76.28

If you should find one of the items on the above list unsatisfactory, be sure you choose a food with the exact vitamins and minerals as the one you have deleted. The foods on the "emergency storage" list have been chosen because they supply all, or most all, of the needed vitamins and minerals to insure good health in a stress situation.

Nutritive Values of Emergency Storage

Powdered Milk

Powdered milk was chosen because of the protein content. Proteins are present in all living tissues and they are essential to life. They make up more than half of all the organic matter in the human body. Blood carries the all important iron-containing protein, hemoglobin, in red cells and several protein in the fluid (plasma) portion. One 8 oz. cup of powdered milk contains 24 grams of protein—over one-third the minimum daily requirement for an adult male. Powdered milk also contains a trace of fat, 35 gms. of carbohydrate, 879 mgs. calcium, 4 mg. iron, 20 I.U. vitamin A, 24 mg. thiamin, 1.21 mg. riboflavin, 6 mg. niacin, 245 calories and 5 mg. vitamin C in an 8 oz. cup.

Whole Wheat

Whole wheat has been the staff of life for people almost since the beginning of time. Wheat is easily cultivated and stored and can be made into palatable, wholesome, and economical foods. Whole wheat was chosen for the "emergency supply" because of its iron and vitamin E content as well as its protein. Wheat protein is low in the essential amino acid lysine. However, when used with milk, corn, or legumes, it makes a complete protein.

Iron is distributed throughout the body, being a component of essential metabolic enzymes in every cell. The adult human body contains a total of 4 to 5 gm. of iron. Most of this, about 65 to 70 percent is present in the blood as hemoglobin in the red blood cells. Each molecule of hemoglobin can carry four molecules of oxygen and is essential for oxygen transfer in the blood.

Vitamin E

Vitamin E is a valuable vitamin. In order to understand the importance of vitamin E, one must realize that the body uses oxygen in each and every cell. This process is called oxidation and is vital to the formation of energy, repair, and growth of the body. By acting as an anti-oxidant vitamin E moderates the use of oxygen, and helps to keep the metabolic process in balance. Vitamin E also prolongs the life of our red blood cells by reducing the formation of these toxic peroxides which, some researchers feel, can hasten the aging process. Most of the vitamins, minerals and much of the protein are in the aleurone layer of wheat and in the wheat germ. The inner part of the wheat kernel consists chiefly of starch with some protein. If most of the aleurone layer is removed (as in milling of a high degree), very little of the original vitamin and mineral content of the grain is left. Thus about 75 percent of the thiamin, a large part of the protein, iron, B complex and many minerals are lost in the process of making white flour.

The Peanut

The peanut was chosen as a food for the "emergency supply" due to the high quality protein and fat. Peanuts are legumes which are meat substitutes. An average serving of a legume furnishes only about one-third as much protein as an average 3¼ oz. serving of meat. The quality of protein from legumes tends to be inferior to animal protein, except for the proteins of the peanut and soybean. However, legume proteins supplement the proteins of cereal grains when combined with wheat or milk. The addition of small amounts of peanut or soybean flour improves the nutritive value of white or wheat bread.

Nuts also have a relatively high protein content (7-18%), but instead of being rich in starch as legumes, they have a high fat content (roughly 50 to 70%). Soybeans and peanuts, (which are legumes) have both high protein and fat, being more like nuts in this respect than like legumes. Though they are low in water, nuts have a relatively high value. Nut proteins are likely to be deficient in one or more of the essential amino acids but are excellent when supplemented with other proteins.

Tomato Juice

Tomato juice is a rich source of vitamin A and C. The human body cannot store vitamin C; nor can it manufacture it. Therefore, vitamin C must be eaten. Tomatoes hold the vitamin C when they are cooked or canned. Vitamin A, like E and K, is oil-soluble. It is essential for vision. The retina of the eye contains a pigment, visual purple, which is composed of vitamin A and protein. Tomatoes also contain 2 mg. of protein, 10 mg. carbohydrates, 17 mg. calcium and iron, riboflavin, niacin, 39 mg. vitamin C and 1,940 I.U. vitamin A.

There are the vitamins and minerals contained in the "emergency supply". Because the foods in the list contain the necessary vitamins and minerals to maintain a healthy body, do not make any substitutions unless the food you are substituting contains the same vitamins and minerals.

After these emergency supplies have been stored away, concentrate your efforts on purchasing the four basics: *wheat, powdered milk, honey,* and *salt* with *water* and *vitamin C* (100 to 250 mg.) added.

Consider each child as an adult, then expand your supply to include staples such as beans, rice, whole kernel corn, grains, fish, meats, fruits, and vegetables. Add nuts and juices to further augment your menus.

The list contained at the end of this chapter is a guide to be used by the novice as well as the experienced to give insight into the weight of and number of foods necessary for a year's supply.

I do not believe each and every item suggested on the list must be purchased. Store only those foods your family enjoys.

Physicians say one can live two months without impairment of health on powdered milk alone. It is suggested that everyone buy powdered milk and learn all about its use. It should be a "must" that every household, especially those with small children, have at least 100 pounds of powdered milk in their supply *immediately*.

Water

In planning your home storage, some water reserve should be considered. The approximate requirement per person on a *two-week* basis is fourteen gallons; seven gallons for drinking and seven gallons for other uses. Storage may be in plastic bottles, to which sodium hypochlorite (bleach) is added. If there is doubt about the purity of the water add one-half teaspoon bleach per five gallons if the water is clear and one teaspoon bleach if the water is cloudy.

In addition, the water contained in water heaters, toilet tanks, and water beds may be used in emergencies. I do not recommend the water in water beds be used for drinking or cooking due primarily to the chemical components used in the manufacture of plastic material. Boiling may remove these harmful toxic chemicals from the water, although there is enough room for doubt that I personally would not use them for these two specific uses. However, the water would still be very valuable and could be used for bathing, washing clothes and dishes or any other use pertaining to the external body uses in a time of major water shortage.

It is recommended that the water heater be drained from time to time to release any accumulated sediment so that the full capacity of the container is readily usable.

When you consider buying wheat for your storage, remember to store only hard red winter wheat with a protein content of 12 percent or above, and a moisture content 10 percent or below. If you have to store white spring wheat remember, when making bread, to add one tablespoonful gluten flour to each cup of spring wheat flour to have enough gluten to make good bread.

Amount of Food to Store for One Year Per Adult

Staples

Wheat, hard winter	700 lbs.	Indefinitely
Unbleached white flour	100 lbs.	1-2 years
Bulgur wheat	100 lbs.	Indefinitely
Wh le kernel corn or corn meal	50 lbs.	5 years
Baking powder	3 lg. boxes	2 years
Cornstarch	3 lg. boxes	5 years
Baking soda	3 lg. boxes	Indefinitely
Oatmeal	25 lbs.	5 years
Honey	1 gallon	Indefinitely
Molasses	1 gallon	Indefinitely
Karo Syrup	1 gallon	Indefinitely
Sugar (Keep dry)	25 lbs.	Indefinitely
Brown Sugar (Keep dry)	10 lbs.	Indefinitely
Shortening	50 lbs.	3 years
Soybean oil	1 gallon	3 years
Peanut oil	1 gallon	3 years
Cocoa	3 lg. boxes	3-5 years
Pero	6 lg. cans	3-5 years
Postum	12 lg. cans	3-5 years
Spaghetti	10 lbs.	5 years
Macaroni	10 lbs.	5 years
Noodles	10 lbs.	5 years
Rice, white	15 lbs.	5 years
Rice, brown	15 lbs.	6-9 months

Protein

Powdered milk	100 lbs.	2-15 years
Mixed Nuts	15 lbs.	1-2 years
Peanuts	15 lbs.	1-2 years
Soybeans	15 lbs.	5 years
Pinto beans	15 lbs.	5 years
Red beans	15 lbs.	5 years

Navy beans	15 lbs.	5 years
Large lima beans	15 lbs.	5 years
Baby lima beans	15 lbs.	5 years
Blackeyed peas	15 lbs.	5 years
Dried green peas	15 lbs.	5 years
Millet	15 lbs.	5 years
Split peas	15 lbs.	5 years
Mung beans	15 lbs.	5 years
Alfalfa seeds—		
Lentils	15 lbs.	5 years
Chia seeds	15 lbs.	5 years
Garbanzo beans	15 lbs.	5 years
Textured vegetable protein (textured soy protein)		5 years
chicken	15 lbs.	5 years
hamburger	15 lbs.	5 years
sausage	15 lbs.	5 years
plain	15 lbs.	5 years
ham	15 lbs.	5 years
bacon	15 lbs.	5 years

Canned Food

Peas	12 jars	3-5 years
Peas and carrots	12 jars	3-5 years
Corn	12 jars	3-5 years
String beans	12 jars	3-5 years
Carrots	12 jars	3-5 years
Tomatoes	12 jars	3-5 years
Spinach	12 jars	3-5 years
Pumpkin	12 jars	3-5 years
Hominy	12 jars	3-5 years
Asparagus	12 jars	3-5 years
Turnip greens	12 jars	3-5 years
Mustard greens	12 jars	3-5 years
Collard greens	12 jars	3-5 years
Sauerkraut	12 jars	3-5 years
Cabbage	12 jars	3-5 years
Cauliflower	12 jars	3-5 years
Onions	12 jars	3-5 years
Chow Chow	12 jars	3-5 years
Pear Relish	12 jars	3-5 years

Pickles	12 jars	3-5 years
Zuccini squash	12 jars	3-5 years
Potatoes and green beans	12 jars	3-5 years

Dried Food—75% Moisture Removed

Prunes	10 lbs.	Indefinitely
Raisins	10 lbs.	Indefinitely
Apples	10 lbs.	Indefinitely
Pears	10 lbs.	Indefinitely
Peaches	10 lbs.	Indefinitely
Apricots	10 lbs.	Indefinitely

Spices and Condiments

Soup base, beef, chicken, ham	6, 1 lb. each	2-3 years
Granulated garlic	1 lb.	2-3 years
Granulated onion	1 lb.	2-3 years
Cayanne pepper	3 lb.	2-3 years
Celery salt	8 oz.	2-3 years
Oregano	8 oz.	2-3 years
Chili powder	8 oz.	2-3 years
Dry mustard	8 oz.	2-3 years
Ginger, ground	8 oz.	2-3 years
Mace, ground	8 oz.	2-3 years
Allspice, ground	8 oz.	2-3 years
Marjoram, ground	8 oz.	2-3 years
Pickling spice	1 lb.	2-3 years
Pumpkin pie spice	8 oz.	2-3 years
Cinnamon sticks	8 oz.	2-3 years
Cinnamon, ground	8 oz.	2-3 years
Nutmeg, ground	8 oz.	2-3 years
Sage, ground	8 oz.	2-3 years
Poultry seasoning	8 oz.	2-3 years
Black pepper	8 oz.	2-3 years
Salt	100 lbs.	Indefinitely
Parsley flakes	1 lb.	2-3 years
Bay leaves	8 oz.	2-3 years
Curry powder	4 oz.	2-3 years
Cloves, ground	4 oz.	2-3 years
Horseradish	4 oz.	2-3 years

Cream tarter	4 oz.	2-3 years
Old Hickory smoked salt	4 oz.	2-3 years
Cumin seed, ground	4 oz.	2-3 years
Tarragon leaves	4 oz.	2-3 years
Vanilla beans	4 oz.	2-3 years
Tumeric, ground	8 oz.	2-3 years
Paprika	1 lb.	2-3 years
Thyme, ground	4 oz.	2-3 years
Rosemary	4 oz.	2-3 years
Cake coloring	2 boxes	2-3 years
Maple flavoring	1 pint	2-3 years
Vanilla flavoring	1 pint	2-3 years
Lemon extract	3 oz.	2-3 years
Peppermint flavoring	3 oz.	2-3 years
Almond extract	3 oz.	2-3 years

Canned Juice

Tomato	12 cans	3-5 years
Pineapple	12 cans	3-5 years
Apple	12 cans	3-5 years
Grapefruit	12 cans	3-5 years

Canned Fruit

Apples	12 jars	3-5 years
Applesauce	12 jars	3-5 years
Apricots	12 jars	3-5 years
Peaches	12 jars	3-5 years
Pears	12 jars	3-5 years
Cherries	12 jars	3-5 years
Blackberries	12 jars	3-5 years
Blueberries	12 jars	3-5 years
Strawberries	12 jars	3-5 years
Rhubarb	12 jars	3-5 years

Dehydrated Food

Protein
Chedder cheese powder	1 can	Indefinitely

Swiss cheese powder	1 can	Indefinitely
Butter powder	1 can	Indefinitely
Peanut butter powder	1 can	Indefinitely
Multi purpose food	1 can	Indefinitely
Egg powder	1 can	Indefinitely

Vegetables

Cut green beans	1 can	Indefinitely
Diced beets	1 can	Indefinitely
Diced cabbage	1 can	Indefinitely
Diced celery	1 can	Indefinitely
Corn	1 can	Indefinitely
Chopped onions	1 can	Indefinitely
Diced potatoes	1 can	Indefinitely
Sliced potatoes	1 can	Indefinitely
Potato granules— mashed	1 can	Indefinitely
Soup blend	1 can	Indefinitely
Spinach flakes	1 can	Indefinitely
Stew blend	1 can	Indefinitely
Tomato crystals	1 can	Indefinitely
Tomato flakes		
Peas, green garden	1 can	Indefinitely

Fruit

Applesauce (plain)	1 can	Indefinitely
Applesauce (Cherry, rasp.)	1 can	Indefinitely
Apple slices	1 can	Indefinitely
Apricot slices	1 can	Indefinitely
Banana flakes	1 can	Indefinitely
Banana slices	1 can	Indefinitely
Date slices	1 can	Indefinitely
Fruit cocktail	1 can	Indefinitely
Fruit mix	1 can	Indefinitely
Peach slices	1 can	Indefinitely
Prunes, pitted	1 can	Indefinitely
Raisins, seedless	1 can	Indefinitely
Tomato flakes	1 can	Indefinitely

Miscellaneous Items

wheat grinder	matches
candles	flash light
wash soap	toilet soap
cleanser	niagra starch
bleach	pencils
toilet tissue	paper napkins
Kleenex, large	first aid kit, large
Wheat for Man cookbook	broom
sanitary napkins	shoe laces
scrubbing brush	transistor radio

Calculating Storage Quantities for Women and Children

Women will eat approximately one-half to three-quarters that consumed by an adult male, teenage males as much as one-half more than the adult male. Teenage females as much as adult females, and consider each child between the ages of 6 and 12 years an adult, children 2-5 years one-half the adult female's allowance, and infants to 2 years one-quarter the adult female allowance.

This list is compiled to assist you in your choice of bulk dry foods, store-bought canned goods or dehydrated foods either separately or in any combination.

RECOMMENDED DAILY DIETARY ALLOWANCES

	Age (years)	G Protein	IU Vit. A	IU Vit. E	Mg. Vit. C	Mg. Iron	Mg. B complex	Energy or Calories
Males	11 - 14	44	5000	12	45	18	3.0	2800
	15 - 22	52	5000	15	45	10	3.0	3000
	23 - 50	56	5000	15	45	10	3.0	2700
	51 +	56	5000	15	45	10	3.0	2400
Females	11 - 14	44	4000	10	45	18	3.0	2400
	15 - 22	48	4000	12	45	18	3.0	2100
	23 - 50	46	4000	12	45	18	3.0	2000
	51 +	46	4000	12	45	10	3.0	1800
Pregnant		+30	5000	15	60	18	4.0	+30
Lactating		+20	6000	15	60	18	4.0	+500
Children	7 - 10	36	3300	10	45	10	2.0	2400
	4 - 6	30	2500	9	45	10	1.5	1800
	1 - 3	23	2000	7	45	15	1.0	1300
Infants	0.0 - 0.5	13.2	1400	14	35	10	0.3	702
	0.5 - 1.0	18.0	2000	5	35	15	0.3	972

Chapter Three

How Should
We Store?

Let us suggest that you set aside a special day to make a *complete* physical inventory of exactly what food and supplies you already have in your cupboards and shelves. Look in every nook and cranny. Don't cheat, list everything! Write it all down! Start to plan your menus to use what you have from what you already have on hand. It might mean eating boiled beans and corn bread every night for a week, and homemade cream of wheat every morning for breakfast, but it will allow you to utilize your regular food budget money to purchase food storage items.

Your first two or three or four orders of storage food should be purchased immediately so that you don't have to purchase groceries. The items purchased should balance and extend the foods which you have inventoried. For example, if you have tuna, noodles and other items for main dishes, then you would want to purchase a can of dehydrated fruit and vegetables. Remember that your meals should be planned and balanced at all times, so if some emergency should arise you would be able to prepare balanced meals. It is unwise to purchase all of your fruits first, or all your vegetables, or all of your meat substitutes.

After you obtain your dehydrated foods, work them into your every day meals. If you would purchase even one can of fruit, one can of vegetables, a meat product, some eggs, and milk, you would be able to have a variety of good meals.

Now every grocery shopping day think—Home Storage! You should habitually order dehydrated or bulk items! Eventually work more and more percentage of your grocery budget into storage and include dehydrated foods in all your meals.

This plan serves two important purposes! It allows you the financial means with which to purchase your storage. Every month systematically order, store and use, until you have reached your goal. Second, you gain experience by trial and error. You learn to measure, season, and cook all of these products. Don't be discouraged; it does take time. If you fail once, always try again; the experience is priceless. Documented studies show over and over again that an emergency is no time to be experimenting with new foods. In some places it is a known fact that children will starve rather than be force-fed a "new" diet. Your entire family could become extremely sick if suddenly they were taken from the "luxury" foods, lacking roughage and vitamins, and put on a 100% wheat diet. It is important to develop your family's taste for the foods you store: Now!

Chapter Four

Where Should We Store?

The most frustrating part of an active Home Storage Program is "Where Should We Store?"

The modern home lacks the pantry or cellar of yesteryear. With some families living in small homes, apartments and mobile homes, storage is a problem. Here are a few simple ideas that may stimulate your own active imagination.

Store your supplies in all the obvious places such as:

1. House—attic, pantry, closets, or try a bedroom wall, hang a chintz curtain, under beds.
2. Garage—add shelving, attic, build storage booths.
3. By adding a cellar, work shop, storage shed, etc.

Personal tastes, lifelong habits, and individual facilities may modify the three answers to a most important facet of Home Storage. Nevertheless, we feel that they are basic as well as sound. We have listed them for consideration as approaches to personal storage problems. To quote the Lord, "If ye be willing and obedient, yet shall eat the good of the land." (Isaiah 1:19)

Chapter Five

The Basic Four

In structuring a storage program of the four basics: wheat, powdered milk, honey, and salt, you must also keep in mind the basic four food groups as a guide to good eating and vibrant health.

BASIC FOUR FOOD GROUPS
[Per Day]

1. **Milk Group**
   3 or more 8 ounce glasses - children
   4 or more 8 ounce glasses - teen-agers
   2 or more 8 ounce glasses - adults
   Cheese, ice cream, and other milk-made foods can supply part of the milk.

2. **Meat Group**
   2 or more servings meat, fish, poultry, eggs, or cheese with dried beans, peas and nuts as alternates.

3. **Vegetables and Fruits**
   4 or more servings—include dark green or yellow vegetables; citrus fruit or tomatoes.

4. **Bread and Cereals**
   4 or more servings—enriched or whole grains, added milk improves nutritional value.

The three chief energy nutrients in the body are carbohydrates, fats and proteins. They are oxidized in the cells by means of oxygen brought to the tissues by the blood, and energy is liberated as heat and work.

We are giving you, the reader, a crash course in nutrition for your benefit in storing the proper foods in proper combinations to give you and your family as healthful a diet as possible. In a survival situation where "stress" is prevalent in all family members, good health is an absolute must.

Your body needs protein each day for construction and repairing body cells. Wheat and gluten made from wheat is a good source of protein. However, wheat is low in the essential amino acid, Lysine, therefore when supplemented with foods high in this substance, wheat and wheat gluten become excellent sources of protein. Foods high in Lysine are milk, Textured Soy Protein (T.S.P.), or Textured Vegetable Protein (T.V.P.), and dry beans.

One-half pound wheat provides the following: 30 grams protein, over 1 milligram of thiamin, 8 milligrams niacin, 6 milligrams iron, some riboflavin and other nutrients.

Take the utmost care in planning your food for storage to insure you provide all the life-giving properties to yourself and your family.

Part 2
Food Storage Facts

Chapter Six

Fumigation is a Must

If there are only three things that may be gleaned from this book about preserving bulk foods, they would be:

1. fumigate
2. Fumigate
3. FUMIGATE!!!

There are many myths and misconceptions concerning "to or not to fumigate." EVERY food item except sugar, powdered milk, salt, and honey MUST BE FUMIGATED with an acceptable method of fumigation to protect your food from becoming infested with weevils or spoilage.

There are several varieties of weevil such as the saw toothed grain beetles, larder beetles, flour beetles, weevils, several kinds of moths, and cockroaches. Many of these are very injurious, especially as larvae, to nuts, fruit and grain.

Under the proper atmosphere these larvae eat the germ or life-giving properties of grains so there is none of the vitamins or other nutrients left to sustain life. Therefore, we strongly urge all who have bulk foods that have not taken the time to FUMIGATE to do so immediately. In case Mr. What's His Name or Mrs. Whatchamacallit have food that has been stored away for X number of years without becoming infested with larvae, we say to you, "it has no larvae, in spite of not being fumigated, not because it wasn't."

There are two acceptable methods of fumigating your bulk foods. However, always keep in mind that the life-giving properties of your grains must, at all costs, be preserved. We realize you may use the fumigating agent of your choice and we make these suggestions for your health and convenience.

The Dry Ice Method

Place a handful of grain or other food in bottom of container; place one or two cubic inches of dry ice on top of it. Pour the remaining grain or other food on top of the dry ice. Fill the container and leave two inches headspace in each can. DO NOT PLACE THE LID ON THE CONTAINER UNTIL THE DRY ICE HAS COMPLETELY DISSIPATED, A MINIMUM OF ONE HOUR, or a serious explosion will result. Dry ice, which is carbon dioxide (CO_2), is an inert gas under these conditions and is non-injurious to these products. After the dry ice has dissipated, place the lid on the container and seal it. Masking tape, hot paraffin wax or bees wax could be used on the cans to keep them airtight. All containers should be labeled with the items contained therein, the date stored, and any other pertinent information. This can be done by putting labels on the cans using masking tape or a grease pencil.

The Sulphur Method

Sulphur, pure rock sulphur, comes in two sizes: the large rock size or the smaller pieces the size of pea gravel. It does not matter which size you use. However, the smaller pieces tend to emit more fumes than the larger pieces.

Different quantities of sulfur are used for various can sizes:

Four or five gallon can — 1 oz. (1 T.) sulphur
Thirty-three gallon garbage can — 6 oz. (6 T.) sulphur
Fifty-five gallon can — 12 oz. (12 T.) sulphur

Place the proper proportion of sulphur in cheesecloth, a clean nylon stocking, or any other material that is porous, in order for the fumes to spread throughout the grain or product to be fumigated. Tie the sulphur in the material used and fill the can. Push the bag of sulphur as far down into the grain as possible. There is no need to wait; the lid may be placed on can immediately.

Apply masking tape around the lid, making sure the can is airtight. Label the can and store it away as usual.

Note: Flowers of sulphur found in most drug stores may be used. However, extreme care should be used due to the fine powder texture of this product. It will not harm the human body if taken internally in small amounts, but bread or any other food with sulphur ground into the flour will have a very unpleasant taste.

Chapter Seven

The Storage Environment

The ideal storage temperature is above forty and below sixty degrees Fahrenheit. Food may be stored in a higher temperature range but higher temperatures decrease shelf life.

Three temperatures are critical to the storage of food. First, some foods will be damaged if they are frozen. Second, above 48°F. most insects become active. The third critical temperature is the temperature at which fats melt—about 95°F.

In general, the lowest temperature short of freezing should be used in storing most foods. Perhaps 40°F. to 60°F. should be the goal, but no temperatures higher than 70°F. should be allowed.

If your storage is kept in a garage or other area where rodents can enter, sprinkle rock sulphur around all cracks, nooks and crannies. This will keep rodents away.

If the floor or your storage area is concete or plain dirt, place slats of lumber between the cement or dirt and the cans to prevent the cans from sweating or rusting.

Always keep in mind the three elements that will destroy your food supply are:
1. Heat
1. Air
3. Moisture

Any combination of the above three elements can do serious damage to your food storage program.

Chapter Eight

Storage Containers

Many different storage containers are available that can keep your food storage safe from air and moisture. However, here are a few helpful hints in selecting your storage containers.

The most important thing you should remember is that you must have a non-porous storage container. Whenever plastic jars or buckets are used, a plastic bag should be used inside them to create a non-porous container. You can use clear or white plastic bags made by "Glad," which is a registered trademark of the

UNION CARBIDE CORPORATION
Home & Automotive Products Division
270 Park Avenue
New York, New York 10017

Most other bags contain chemicals that may emit harmful fumes into the foods if used for long term shortage. Put the plastic bag in the jar or bucket, fill it with wheat, fumigate, then tape the lid and label the jar or bucket.

Fifty-five gallon metal cans may be used with great success. These do not need a plastic bag insert nor do the lids need to be taped, since most have self-lock rims.

If you choose to use large plastic garbage cans, make absolutely certain a very wide tape is used to tape the lid to the can. This is necessary to keep rodents and all other insects from crawling between the lid and can causing your food to be either infested or contaminated.

Glass gallon jars or any other container of the same type may be safely used in your food storage program.

Chapter Nine

Shelving and Rotation

Rotate your perishables! You cannot keep a year's supply *on hand* or successfully store canned or bottled foods without spoilage unless you faithfully follow a rotation plan. Here are two methods which have been used successfully:

Method 1.

1. A good system is to build some shelves of 1" x 12" lumber, spacing the shelves wide enough apart to stack two #2½ size cans with an inch or two to spare. The 12" board will hold a surprising amount of cans.

2. Purchase a grease pencil and mark each article or can with the date of purchase, showing the month and year (e.g. 2/6 for February 1976).

3. Divide your storage shelves into allotted space for each type of food, allowing one extra row for rotation for each variety.

For example, you can put six #2½ size cans in a row on a 12" board, stacked two high and three deep. Thus if you were storing 24 cans of tomatoes, you would have four rows with six cans in a row. Leave the fifth row empty. The storage shelf would then look like this: showing top view of cans stacked 2 high).

Row:	A	B	C	D	E
	O	O	O	O	
	O	O	O	O	
	O	O	O	O	12" board

4. Store the oldest dates in row A, next oldest in row B, etc. The new replacement purchased will be put in the empty row E, explained next.

5. You are now ready to rotate. Since row A contains the oldest stock, you first remove for use from row A. For each and every can removed, purchase another as soon as possible and stack in row E, after dating each can with the month and year. By doing this you will have row E filled at the time you have emptied row A. You then begin using out of row B, putting newly purchased stock in row A. This way you will always have one row being emptied while you are filling another, and you can maintain your storage up-to-date, complete and "on hand for at least a year ahead."

Method 2.

1. This is a slanting-shelf to allow cans to roll to the low end of the shelf. Replacement purchases will be put in at the high end of the shelf, thus allowing the oldest stock to be removed from the low end.

2. Each article should be marked with date of purchase as indicated in method 1.

3. Slanting shelves can be made any length and height as long as both ends are easily accessible. Construct them according to these guidelines:

    A. Slant the shelf one inch for each linear foot of shelf.

    B. Space the 3/8 inch guides carefully the entire length of the shelf so the cans will roll freely without binding.

    C. Spaced between shelves according to the size of cans to be used on each shelf.

    D. Vertical supports should be spaced no more than three feet apart.

    E. List of materials:
        #1 shelves 1" x 12"
        #2 support 1" x 2"
        #3 guides 3/8" x 1"
        #4 ends 3/8" x 1"

From the Book
Gateway to Survival is Storage
by Walter D. Batchelor, Copyright 1968
by Walter D. Batchelor. Used with permission.

Note: In case you do not wish to use either of these methods you can just stack your cans one on top of the other, leaving room for air to circulate around the cans.

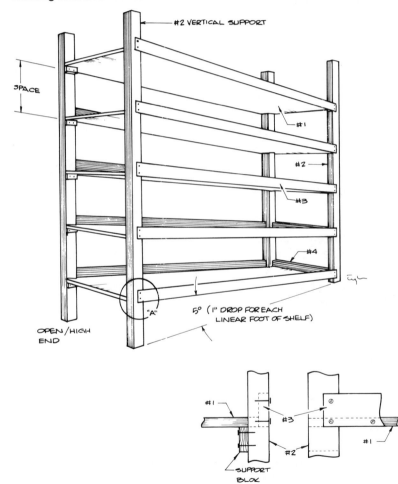

DETAIL "A"

The shelf life of your food supply depends entirely on how well you followed the instructions in Chapter Six *Fumigation is a Must* and Chapter Eight *Storage Containers*. It stands to reason that if your food is properly canned, fumigated, rotated, and if the storage temperature is as constant as you can provide, you will achieve the maximum shelf life for your storage area.

Shelf Life of Your Year's Supply

Short Rotations   *Years*

grapefruit juice.. 1-2
orange juice.. 1-2
cherries... 1-2
berries.. 1-2
prunes... 1-2
plums.. 1-2
catsup... 2
margarine.. 9-12 mo.
    (no lard in ingredients)
yeast.. 2
flour (white).. 1-2
cheese (frozen).. 1-2
cheese (vinegar cloth)................................. 1-2
brown rice... 1
dried fruit (not dehydrated)........................... 1-2
baking powder.. 2
canned milk (must be turned upside down every thirty..... 1-2
    days) rotated

Longer Rotations   *Years*

salmon... 4
tuna... 4
deviled meats.. 4
canned vegetables...................................... 4
canned fruit... 3-8
bottled fruit (with the exception of highly acid or
    pigmented food or those with pits................... 3-9
vegetable oil.. 3
corn oil... 3

corn oil. 3
canned shortening. 2
   (no lard)
peanut butter. 2

Indefinite or Five Years

hard winter wheat	white rice
whole kernel corn	honey
dehydrated onions	macaroni
spaghetti	salt
lasagna	soda
Sugar	lentils
beans; navy, lima, pinto and soy	

Part 3

Back
To
Basics

Chapter Ten

Dehydration

There are three main ways to dehydrate food: under the sun, in the oven, or in either a homemade or store-bought dehydrator. Many people wonder about the art of dehydrating foods, which is not a new technique. Our great-grandfathers used to sun-dehydrate their food seventy-five years ago as one of their few means of food preservation. With modern technology it still remains one of the best means of preserving food.

The art of dehydrating food opens a new and marvelous awareness of the rich sweet taste of fresh garden vegetables. In the dehydrating process the temperature used to dehydrate fruit and vegetables is very low, a mere 110 to a maximum of 117 degrees F. This low temperature is used to retain all the life-giving vitamins and nutrients that are normally destroyed by high heat.

To dehydrate properly, fruits and vegetables are harvested at the very peak of maturity and then rushed to the dehydrators and dehydrated at 110 degrees F. The dehydrating process, depending upon the fruit or vegetable used, takes between 18 and 36 hours. The vegetables are washed and sorted to remove any damaged or overripe fruit. These are set aside to be used in fruit and vegetable leathers. Any combination of fruits or vegetables may be used in making leathers. Nothing need be thrown away except the pits and peelings.

Dehydrated Foods Taste Best

One interesting facet of the dehydrating process is the taste of fruits and vegetables that have been rehydrated after being dehydrated. These foods have a new and exciting taste found only in home grown produce harvested fresh when both flavor and nutrition are the very best. Fruits have a natural sweetness that most people who have been raised in the city have never experienced. Fruits purchased from the produce section of your local supermarket have been harvested green, stored in the cold storage refrigerator of the grower for from several days to several weeks, then shipped to the wholesaler or distributor, and then on to the produce section of the market. Harvesting fruits and vegetables in this way takes its toll on the rich flavor and vitamin content.

Flavor Retained

The flavor of dehydrated food is retained because the large companies contract several years ahead from the farmer for certain vegetables. These are vine-ripened at the very peak of maturity when the flavor is the very best, then rushed to the dehydrating companies to be dehydrated. This process removes ninety-eight percent of the water, while retaining nearly all the vitamins, flavor and color. When dehydrated, some vegetables shrink between one-seventh to one-eighth of their normal size. For example:

It takes twelve pounds of fresh green beans to yield one pound of dehydrated green beans.

Fourteen pounds of carrots are needed to yield one pound of dehydrated carrots.

Six pounds dry aged chedder cheese will yield one pound dehydrated chedder cheese.

Freeze-Dried Food

Since most housewives are unfamiliar with dehydrated food, they are also unfamiliar with freeze-dried foods and tend to confuse the two. Freeze-dried foods are similar to dehydrated foods in that they are harvested at the very peak of maturity. Here the process changes. The fruit or vegetables are rushed to freezing units and are quick-frozen. After this they are rushed to the dehydrators and are then dehydrated at the same low temperature as dehydrated foods. However, there is a vast difference between freeze-dried and dehydrated food.

Vegetables, like peas, for example, when dehydrated look like little green withered glumps. After they are rehydrated by bringing them to a boil and then simmering for 10-15 minutes, they look and taste like peas fresh from grandmother's garden. They are green, plump and have a natural sweetness that is truly surprising.

Unopened dehydrated foods will last indefinitely. Once opened, cover them with a plastic lid and they will stay up to three years on your pantry shelf.

Freeze-dried foods, unlike dehydrated foods, retain their cellular structure and do not shrink as much as dehydrated foods. As an example, freeze-dried strawberries look like miniature strawberries. Freeze-dried foods yield considerably less servings per can and cost considerably more. Like dehydrated food, freeze-dried foods will last indefinitely unopened. However, once opened, they must be used within five to seven days like fresh food, or it will spoil.

Wet Pack Food

Research shows there is a monetary advantage in storing dehydrated food as well as a nutritional one. These low moisture fruits and vegetables are light weight and compact for ease in storing. The cost per serving is half that of wet pack foods. When preparing meals with dehydrated foods, you do not have to cut, peel, dice, slice, shred, cut off the bad spots or pour off the water. Everything in the can is good edible food; nothing is wasted. It is not so with wet pack foods. Again, research shows that the label on brand X whole kernel corn states that the contents weigh 16 ounces and costs $.49 per can. Further examination reveals the corn weighs 8 ounces, and the liquid also weighs 8 ounces. Corn and liquid each costs $.24½. The liquid, however, is poured down the drain in the kitchen sink at a loss of $.24½. Researchers have said many times, "If it were human, the kitchen sink drain would be the most healthy human in the world." Researchers say this, I am sure, because of the amount of vegetable liquid homemakers pour down the kitchen sink drain containing valuable vitamins and minerals.

We therefore strongly suggest that everyone store dehydrated and freeze-dried foods in the amounts with which they feel comfortable due to the economy and weight factor as well as the flavor and appeal that these foods will bring into your meals.

Fruit Leather Recipes

Fruit leather can be made from many types of fruits. To make fruit leather, pour all ingredients in the blender and blend until smooth. Pour onto dehydrator trays lined with Glad plastic wrap ¼ inch from the top. Dehydrate approximately 24 hours. When fully dehydrated, the fruit texture will be soft, pliable, and slightly sticky.

Place a piece of Glad plastic wrap on the counter top, cut fruit leather in half, lay it on the Glad wrap and roll like a jelly roll. Place it on a container with a tight-fitting lid.

Apple Banana
4 cups apples
2 cups bananas
½ cup honey

Apple Berry
4 cups apples
2 cups berries
½ cup honey

Berry Apple Peach
4 cups berries
1 cup apples
1 cup peaches

Peach Apricot
4 cups peaches
2 cups apricots
½ cup honey

Peach Apple Banana
2 cups peaches
1 cups apples
1 cup banana
1 cup pineapple
½ cup honey

Pineapple Apple Peach
2 cups pineapple
1 cup apples
1 cup peaches
1 cup apricots
½ cup honey

Apricot
2 cups apricots
1 cup peaches
1 cup apples
½ cup banana
½ cup honey

Banana
2 cups bananas
½ cup peaches
½ cup apricots
½ cup pineapple
½ cup honey

Pear Apple
2 cups pears
2 cups apples
½ cup honey

Pineapple Berry
2 cups pineapple
1 cup berries
½ cup honey

Cherry Pineapple
2 cups pitted cherries
1 cup pineapple
1 cup peaches
1 cup apricots
½ cup honey

Cherry Berry
2 cups raspberries
2 cups pitted cherries
1 cup strawberries
1 cup blueberries
½ cup honey

Strawberry Cherry
2 cups strawberries
1 cup pitted cherries
½ cup honey

Banana Strawberry
2 cups bananas
1 cup strawberries
½ cup honey

Strawberry Peach
2 cups strawberries
1 cup peaches
½ cup honey

Peach Banana
2 cups peaches
1 cup banana
½ cup honey

Banana
4 cups bananas
½ cup honey

Strawberry
4 cups strawberries
½ cup honey

Apple Cinnamon
4 cups apples
½ tsp. cinnamon
½ cup honey

Peach
4 cups peaches
¼ tsp. nutmeg
½ cup honey

Apricot
4 cups apricots
½ cups honey

Pear
4 cups pears
½ cup honey

Dehydrated Food More Economical than Canned Food

For example:
One case of No. 303 cans equals 24 cans. One case of wet pack product would cost approximately the same as No. 10 can of the same item in dehydrated form. With the dehydrated

product you do not pay for the water, seeds, peelings, or bad spots, just the product without any waste.

Suppose you've allotted $5.00 for your storage budget this month to buy fruit cocktail. The supermarket has brand x, No. 303 can on sale at 5/$1.00. This is a very good price. You bring home 25 cans. When drained and measured the amount of fruit per can is approximately 1 cup, this will give you 25 cups.

In contrast, one No. 10 can dehydrated fruit mix weighs 44 ounces. One cup equals 4 ozs. dry weight. One can contains 11 cups dry. However, when the water is returned to the product, there will be approximately 33 cups of fruit.

From the book *Just Add Water*
by Barbara G. Salsbury
published by Horizon Publishers
Bountiful, Utah. Copyright 1972,
by Horizon Publishers. Used by permission.

Dehydrated foods, depending upon the fruit or vegetables, shrink to one-seventh or one-eighth of their normal size. The cost of a three-ounce serving of dehydrated food is 2.5 cents compared to 5.3 cents per three-ounce serving of wet pack food.

Oven dehydrating can be an enjoyable event for the entire family. Prepare fruit or vegetables by slicing them thin (cut scant ¼" slices), place them on cookie sheets, turn the oven on at the lowest possible setting, and put the cookie sheets into the oven. Leave the oven door open ½" for electric ovens and eight inches for gas ovens. Stir occasionally till completely dry (between twelve and twenty-four hours).

Sun-drying. A surprising variety of foods can be sun-dried—especially produce, which should be chosen for top quality, picked over, and washed. Juicy fruits are usually halved or quartered and vegetables, which are low in acid and spoil more readily, cut into small pieces for faster dehydration.

Many people then dry their produce without further ado, and enjoy good success. Some experts on food preservation, though, hold that vegetables should first be blanched in scalding steam to stop the action of enzymes that cause deterioration in storage. Another pre-treatment—exposure to the fumes of burning sulfur—is often advised for fruits such as apples, apricots, peaches and pears, to preserve color and vitamins A and C. **Caution:** If and when sulfur is burned for any reason use **extreme care.** Sulfur, when burned, emits a **poisonous gas, sulfur dioxide,** a heavy, pungent, toxic gas that is easily condensed to a colorless liquid.

Treated or not, the foods are spread without crowding on paper-lined trays or preferably cloth-covered wooden frames, protected with cheesecloth if insects are a problem, and left in the sun to dry with the aid of occasional turning. The trays should be moved under shelter in case of rain and guarded from dampness at night.

Chapter Eleven

Fermenting

Fermentation of vegetables is the same type of process as salting and brining. Fermenting vegetables is a simple, inexpensive method for preserving both meat and vegetables. It requires no special equipment, materials or skill. In many rural areas, or when it isn't feasible to freeze, dry, or can, this method is used. And if the electricity supply were cut off for a considerable period this method would be a good way to prevent the spoilage of food in the deep freeze.

Details for fermenting string beans are shown below. Other vegetables suitable for this treatment are:

Cabbage	Turnips
Corn	Vegetable greens
Peas and Lima Beans	Onions
(unshelled)	Cucumbers
Carrots	Green and red peppers
Cauliflower	Beets

In the fermenting of vegetables, bacteria feed on the sugars which are drawn from the vegetable material by salt or brine, and in the process acid is produced.

Directions and precautions. Use any clean container except metal ones—e.g. crocks, wooden barrels, or kegs, glass fruit jars, or plastic buckets.

Equipment
Crock jar (five gallon)
Fruit jars (glass lids)
Plate (or round hardwood
    board)
Weight (water in
    gallon jar)
Cotton cloth (two pieces)

Ingredients
Vegetables
Salt and water
Fresh dill or seeds
Grape leaves
Garlic and pickling spice

1. Pick the string beans when they are small, just as the bean is beginning to form. Older beans will get soft inside and tough outside. Cut in 2-inch pieces. Weigh the beans.

2. Measure the water needed to fill the crock (about 6 to 7 quarts). Divide it equally into two containers.

3. One-half cup of salt (5 ounces) is needed for every 10 pounds of vegetables. Divide the required amount in equal parts and dissolve it in the two containers of water. (Water containing two little salt will make the beans soft instead of snappy and crisp.)

4. In the bottom of the crock place one bunch of fresh dill with seeds attached. (If this is not available, use the seeds from packages.)

5. Fill the crock with several layers of the cut beans and pour salt water over them. When the crock is nearly filled with beans, make a hole in the center and put a handful of garlic (four or five whole garlics, each cut in two). Add one heaping tablespoon of pickling spice. (Mix it throughout the beans with a wooden spoon, or wash hands and arms and mix.

6. Put about four layers of overlapping grape leaves on top and cover the crock with a cotton cloth large enough to hang down over the edge of the crock for a few inches all around.

7. Over the cloth put an inverted plate, or a round hardwood board a little smaller than the crock. Weight it down with a gallon jar containing as much water as needed. Cover it with a clean cloth to keep away gnats, etc.

8. When foam starts building up, skim it off carefully for about four or five days. A greyish or brownish scum comes up on the plate and cloth. If this is not removed it will destroy the fermentation acid and the beans will be soft. To remove the scum, remove the weight and plate, fold the cloth to the

center, take it to the sink, wash it out, and then replace the cloth, plate and weight.

9. Shake the crock. If you hear no bubbling, the fermentation is complete. (It should take from 10 days to 2 weeks, depending on the temperature.) The beans are now ready to put in bottles. When taking them out of the crock or jar, use a fork or a spoon and not the fingers, as you may start a new fermentation in that way. Use glass lids if available, or cellophane and metal ring. Fill jars to the very top with beans and with the juice from the crock so that there is no room for air. Put them in a cool place on layers of paper so that any juice leaking out won't damage the shelf. The beans are delicious with meat instead of pickles.

From the book, *Passport To Survival*
by Esther Dickey, published by Bookcraft.
Copyright 1969 by Bookcraft, Inc.
Used with permission.

Chapter Twelve

Smoking and Curing Meat

Smoked meat has a very palatable flavor. Smoking is a simple process to "dry out" meat. Smoking tends to inhibit bacterial action. Cool smoked meats need no refrigeration. If electricity should go off for a long period of time, meats in frozen storage could be thawed and smoked for preservation.

Most kinds of meat can be smoked—hams, fish, wild game, beef, lamb, turkey, chicken, and fresh homemade sausage stuffed in narrow muslin bags. Tougher cuts make good jerky: cut along the grain, not across it.

Types of smokers include: small building, wooden barrel, box, ice box, refrigerator, or a portable smoker from the sporting goods store that fits in the fireplace. Take care to make the smoker fire-resistant by lining the lower half with metal or asbestos. Holes to control ventilation and temperature are needed. Use a thermometer, and keep the temperature at 90 degrees. The meat can either be hung from hooks or spread out in small pieces on wire trays. Allow a 2-inch clearance around the sides of the smoker for circulation of air. (Excerpts from the book, *Passport To Survival*, by Esther Dickey, published by Bookcraft. Copyright 1969 by Bookcraft, Inc. Used with permission.)

Another item that can be successfully used for a smoker is an old water heater with a door cut in the front and replaced with hinges and a handle. This is used for the fire box. A small rack is used, a fire is built under the rack, and a can or cast iron skillet is used for the wet chips. The top is measured four inches from the top toward the bottom. This section is cut off and replaced with hinges to make a lid. Another rack is placed inside, where the meat is placed for either barbecuing or smoking. (See diagram.)

Curing meat with salt is an old technique used many years ago before farmers had the convenience of modern day refrigeration.

Hams, shoulders, and middlin meat were the pieces most commonly cured. These pieces were taken to the smoke house as soon after slaughtering as possible, preferably while the meat was still warm, and never more than twenty-four hours after.

The meat was taken to the smokehouse, thoroughly salted, and then set upon waist-high shelves or down in boxes or barrels to "take the salt". Most people preferred the shelf system, as it allowed the meat to get the necessary ventilation more easily. Meanwhile, the winter weather provided natural refrigeration while the meat was going through the curing process.

To Cure Meat

After the animal is washed and cleaned thoroughly, cut it into four or six pieces, for ease in handling. Rub salt into each piece until well covered (about 8-10 pounds per hundred pounds of meat). Wrap in cheese cloth and put it on a shelf or leave unwrapped and put in barrel or box.

For a different taste, a mixture of one or two quarts of honey or molasses, two ounces black pepper, and two ounces red pepper can be mixed with the salt and brushed on the meat. Leave on six to eight weeks, or longer if the weather is cold. Whenever you want meat, unwrap it, cut what you need, and rewrap it each time.

In the spring, fire up the smokehouse, box or barrel. Thoroughly wash salt or salt-molasses mixture off meat and smoke as usual.

Excerpts from the Book,
Passport To Survival, by Esther Dickey,
published by Bookcraft. Copyright 1969
by Bookcraft, Inc. Used with permission.

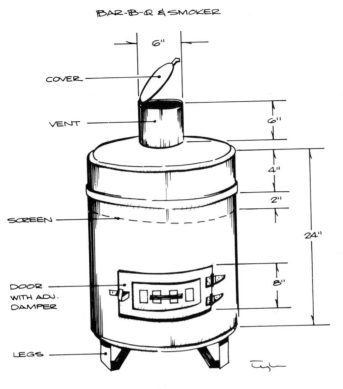

BAR-B-Q & SMOKER

THIS BAR-B-Q & SMOKER CAN BE
MADE FROM A 30 OR 40 GAL. ELECT.
WATER HEATER TANK. J.D. Mason.

Pemmican [The Indian Method of Preserving Meat]

Cut the lean meat into very thin slices. Hang in the sun where flies and dirt cannot get to it and allow it to dry thoroughly. Strips of meat may be dried by suspending the strips over a low fire made of hickory or ash wood until brittle. There are a variety of ways the meat may be dried so use your imagination. Drying may take from a few hours to a day, depending on the climate. Pound or grind the dry strips of meat into a coarse powder and work in enough hot fat (optional) to make a thick dough, form into loaves and wrap.

Here is where the Indian people differ in the making of Pemmican, their main staple diet, which they made during the summer when deer, buffalo and berries were abundant. It was to be stored away for their winter food whenever these ingredients became scarce and hunger was around the corner. Instead of using hot fat, which is fuel for the body, the Indians powdered meat, berries, and corn. Then, taking a rawhide pouch, they layered the meat, corn and berries, tied the pouch securely, and set it aside in a cool dry place. In case of an attack on their village by a hostile tribe, the first thing the squaws would grab were the rawhide pouches of Pemmican.

Chapter Thirteen

Brine-Curing Meat

Begin a couple of days after slaughter (after meat has been chilled from 32 degrees to 34 degrees). For the brine cure for 100 pounds of meat you will need:

  8 pounds salt
  2 pounds white or brown sugar
  2 ounces of saltpeter

Dissolve the ingredients in 6 gallons of cold water. Pack the chilled, trimmed meat carefully and closely in a clean crock or other container and pour in cold brine (36 to 38 degrees) until the pack begins to shift and float. Weight it down. Overhaul the meat in 3 to 5 days—that is, repack it so that all pieces are exposed to brine. Thin cuts of meat take from 10 days to 2 weeks, legs and shoulders from 25 to 40 days.

Part 4

Non-Food Necessities

Chapter Fourteen

Medical Supplies

Families have an essential role in a survival situation, a role that is both simple and complex. In a survival situation, every family member must be ready to live on his own for a period of time when outside assistance might not be available.

The importance of this role becomes readily apparent when one appreciates the fact that the ability of the family to continue to survive and to cope with an emergency situation depends entirely upon the preparations it makes **before** the emergency.

Your problem and responsibility would be to maintain health without outside help. The purpose of this chapter is to assist you in meeting that responsibility.

This chapter is not intended as a substitute for professional medical care. It is intended only to help in maintaining health and alleviating suffering during any period of emergency when professional care and normal services might not be available.

Some of the preparations you can make for the health of your family in an emergency are as simple as they are important. For example, there are certain supplies you should have on hand. You should make sure that all vaccinations, such as smallpox, tetanus shots and others recommended by your physician, are kept up to date for all members of the family. These and other preparations should be made now, because there would not be time to do them in an emergency.

Medical and First Aid Supplies

Medical supplies must be tailored to the individual needs of your family. Existing health problems in the family, such as diabetes, heart disease, asthma, or peptic ulcer, may make it necessary to include certain specific medicines in your supply.

If there are infants or children in your family, you may need such things as baby aspirin and vaseline. If anyone in the family is pregnant, you must be prepared with supplies for emergency delivery and after-care of mother and child. (See **Expectant Mother's Emergency Childbirth Kit.**) Elderly members of the family may have special needs.

In addition to special items dictated by family health problems and by the age of the family members, there is a basic list of medical and first-aid supplies recommended for all. You are urged to discuss this basic list, as well as your special needs, with your doctor so that he may suggest specific medicines to buy, provide you with prescriptions, if necessary, and advise you regarding quantities you will need. He can also tell you how to use the medicines, how to store them, and how long they can be stored without significant deterioration.

It is suggested that 5-gallon cans be used to store basic medical supplies. This will insure dryness and also the antiseptic qualities of some supplies.

Medicine obtained for your emergency supply should be so labeled that the name of the medicine, instructions for use, and necessary warnings, such as "for external use only" and "poison," are clearly visible. These medicines should be carefully packed to prevent breakage. They should be stored out of reach of children in a dry, cool place. Best storage temperature should be below 70 degrees F., but they should not be frozen. Remember to rotate your medicines, and to date and label cans with contents.

A well-run household will always have a certain amount of medicines and bandages on hand. If you would see to it that you have on hand a little more than "normal amounts" of those items listed below, you would have a good start toward your year's emergency medical supplies.

Let us list those things you probably have on hand:

First aid book

Box of assorted band-aids

Sterile 4" x 4" pads

Adhesive tape, 1" wide

Gauze

Roll cotton, one pound

Sheets and towels (for slings and dressings)

Splints, matches, and candles

Q-tips

Sharp knife and razor blades

Ace bandages 2", 3" and 4"

Scissors

Vaseline, in one-pound jars

Tweezers

Antibiotic ointment (neosporin)

Eye dropper

Murine, or other eye wash

Eye glass, to wash eyes

Boric Acid crystals, powder and ointment to make eye wash

Oral and Rectal thermometer

Epsom Salts (to reduce swelling sprains and strains)

Erogophene Ointment (drawing salve), 8 or 12 oz. size

Oil of Cloves (toothache drops)

Ethyl Alcohol 70% (rubbing and sterilizing)

Hot water bottles

Tourniquet (belt will do)

Ice pack

Flashlight

Black silk thread, (for suturing— use any thread in emergency)

Bed pan

Measuring cup and spoons

Iodine

Hydrogen Peroxide

Tincture of Green Soap

Baking Soda

Merthiolate

Dry mustard (induces vomiting)

Table Salt

Syrup of Ipecac (induces vomiting for poisoning

Cornstarch (for scalding or chaffing)

Kaopectate (for diarrhea)

Cayenne pepper (cuts, sore throat, ulcers)

Needles, safety pins

Metholatum

Milk of Magnesia

Olive oil (for consecrating)

Purex

Paregoric (see your doctor for a prescription)

Aspirin or A.P.C.'s (Name-brand Upjohn Libby: Others break down.) 1000 tablet size. Ask your druggist to order them for you.

Vitamins, multipurpose and singles C,D, and E.

Especially store any medication your family may need for particular ailments. You may also want to add a few things that are stable in large quantities.

Farmers Like:
Bag Palm for animals and wounds, scratches for themselves
Petro Carbo Salve (for man or beast)
Carbolated Vaseline

A universal antidote can be purchased in redimixed foil packets for instant use which contains Tannic Acid, Milk of Magnesia (Magnesium Hydroxide) and activated charcoal. In an emergency burnt toast can furnish the charcoal, tea, a source of Tannic Acid, and Milk of Magnesia can be used for the Magnesium Hydroxide (see first aid book).

Butesin Picrate ointment is excellent for burns. It contains an anesthetic and other healing properties and may be purchased in one pound jars.

Perma Pac, Sam Andy, and Neo Life multi-purpose vitamins packaged for long term storage are a good idea if food supplies get tight. By all means gear your medical storage to your family's physical health.

"Expectant Mother's Emergency Childbirth Kit"

These items must be as sterile as possible before storing away in a special box marked "Expectant Mother's Emergency Childbirth Kit" with contents clearly labeled.

1. Black silk thread—for suturing
2. Scissors
3. Tweezers, assorted needles
4. Surgical soap, Tincture Green Soap
5. Clean box, for storage of equipment, and baby's basket
6. Clean clothes for infant
7. Blankets, sheets for box
8. Baby oil
9. One pound roll cotton
10. Hot water bottle
11. Sanitary napkins or clean rags
12. Sanitary belt—or safety pins
13. Bottles, nipples, 2 each
14. Black heavy duty thread, twine or shoe string (for typing the umbilical cord)

15. Syringe rubber or a nasal aspirator (to remove mucus from baby's throat)

16. Lots of clean newspapers, to be used as padding for mother and infant's bed.

How to Tie an Umbilical Cord

These brief instructions are most important to the inexperienced delivering a baby without professional medical help.

1. After the baby is born, lay him on his mother's stomach, with his head hanging down.

2. Tie the cord about 2" from infant's stomach. *Do not* tie it until the umbilical cord *stops pulsating,* then tie it by wrapping twine or shoestring around the cord four times.

3. Tie it again about 2" from the first tie, away from the baby's stomach, again making four wraps around the cord.

4. Make sure each tie closes off the cord securely. Take care not to cut the cord with the twine or string.

5. Cut the cord *between* the two ties.

6. Hand the infant to the person who is assisting, or if you are alone, immediately wrap baby in a blanket. Put on a cap, or cover on his head, and lay him beside his mother. Finish taking care of the mother, then follow the instructions at the end of this chapter.

If you ever have to deliver a baby in an emergency situation you will profit from these helpful suggestions on what to do and the equipment needed.

First, don't *panic!* Keep calm, Mother Nature has a way of doing things. All you need do is assist her. If you stay calm the expectant mother will be calm.

Make absolutely certain you and everyone who is going to assist by handling the baby has first washed their hands with surgical soap, Tincture of Green Soap, or plain soap for three or four minutes. Make sure fingernails are also clean.

Care of the New Infant

Nothing should be done to the baby's eyes, ears, nose, or mouth. The baby should not be cleaned in any way the first day. He will be covered with a thin, white waxy material. This material will be unpleasant looking and will soon have an unpleasant odor. However, it acts as a protective covering for the baby's skin and will protect it against infection better than any cleaning. It also helps the baby adjust to the change in temperature between the mother's womb and the outside world. At this point it is vital the new baby be kept *warm*.

The newborn baby needs very little care during the first few days of life. He can get along without food or water for two days or longer, if necessary.

After twenty-four hours the baby can be bathed. Baby oil may be used if water is scarce. Sterile dressings should be used on the stump of the cord at the navel until the cord dries up and falls off, usually within one week. Make absolutely certain the baby is kept warm. This is vital to the life of the baby. Put a hat, cap, a pieces of cotton cloth, or a diaper on the baby's head as quickly after he is born as possible. It has been discovered newborn babies lose vital body heat through their heads.

Chapter Fifteen

Clothing, Material, and Patterns

Sufficient durable clothing also should be included in a home storage program to take care of the requirements of a family for at least a years' time. This clothing should accommodate the needs for the different seasons. Sturdy work or walking boots for each family member should be included in your storage preparations. Make certain they are well "broken in". A survival situation is not the time for blisters or sore aching feet.

It is wise also to store fabrics, such as a heavy denim for work clothes, thread, needles and other sewing items. The provident housewife will take advantage of sales of materials suitable for making the clothes her family may require and store her purchases until such time as they are needed. Savings are also possible in keeping clean, used clothing on hand which can be remodeled, cut down for a younger member of the family, or refurbished.

A bolt of cotten flannel, for baby, one of unbleached muslin, for making sheets, and one of cotton print for shirts and dresses should also be stored away.

Many modern women today have forgotten how to sew by hand. Home sewing skills should be strengthened in every household if they are not adequate to meet family needs in an emergency situation.

Here is a suggested list of sewing notions for your survival sewing basket.

Sewing Notions

needles—hand
needles—machine, tredle
straight pins
safety pins
thimble
tape measure
pin cushion
scissors
zippers
hooks and eyes
snaps
buttons
bias tape
lace

rick rack
zippers—heavy coat
machine oil
knitting needles
yarn
quilting frames
patterns (family)
gripper tool
extra belt (tredle machine)
buckles
batting
elastic
patching material
ribbon

Chapter Sixteen

Baby Box

Babies have a way of coming, sometimes quite unexpectantly, and sometimes in emergency situations. Families with babies on the way should have a baby box in which they accumulate the necessary paraphernalia for the newborn child.

In preparing your "baby box" you may have on hand some infant clothing that would do very well. Take a physical inventory of everything you have on hand from your last baby. Mend and wash these items and check them off the list you prepared from your inventory. Next start accumulating the things on your list, adding to your "baby box" each week, or month. Clothes need not always be purchased new; watch the garage sales, second hand shops and thrift stores for good used clothing. Store them with moth balls, label and date.

The following items will be needed for a baby from birth till the age of four months:

gowns, cotton—12	baby aspirin
under shirts—12	thermometer—rectal
diapers—3 doz.	enema syringe
sox or booties—6 pr.	bottles
receiving blankets—6	nipples
crib blankets—6	cap or hat
crib sheets—6	crib mattress
crib or large box	Q-tips
sweater—2	cotton

bunting—1
olive oil
baby vitamins
antiseptic solution
boric acid

baby oil
baby powder or cornstarch
baby soap
assorted safety pins
teething lotion

Chapter Seventeen

Bedding

Just as food should be stored against a time of emergency, families should also accumulate sufficient bedding to last a year. It should have sheets, pillow cases, and warm blankets.

However, since modern manufacturing methods have designed the innerspring, posturepedic, king, queen, full, and twin size mattress, most of us have lost sight of what to do without those conveniences. However, the early pioneers brought no mattress, springs or beds along with them. Being forced to improvise, they made their own. Here is how it was done, with several plans that include instructions, and a diagram in case you build your own.

The earliest mattresses were simply bed-sized cloth sacks filled with straw or feathers. These were laid over a rope netting that was attached to a simple, four sided frame with legs. Others were just laid in a corner and brought out at night to be slept in right on the floor.

Instructions

Build a frame with four end posts and four side pieces to the dimensions to fit you. Bore a row of holes through the side pieces, spacing them six inches apart. They should be directly opposite each other on the paired sides, head and foot.

Now you are ready to begin the actual rope weaving. Begin at the headboard and string the bed lengthwise as shown in the diagram. When the last hole in the headboard is filled, bring the rope under and diagonally across to the side of the bed and begin the over and under weaving as shown in the diagram. When the last hole is filled, take the rope underneath the bed frame and tie it securely to one of the laced ropes.

The straw or feather mattress can be laid directly on the ropes. No further support is needed.

To make a straw or feather mattress simply make a "tick"—a bag to be used as a mattress, out of some strong denim or pillow ticking to fit the dimensions of your frame. Fill it with straw or feathers and put it directly on top of ropes. Fluff it every day or so, and air it occasionally.

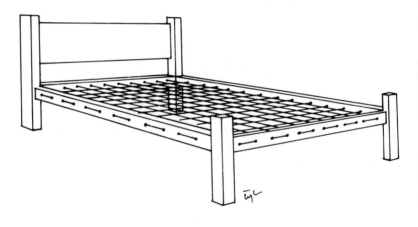

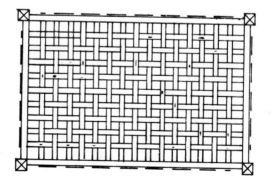

Part 5
Survival
Mechanics

Chapter Eighteen

Baking Without an Oven

Today most people have fireplaces in their homes as an amenity rather than a necessity. Once, however, the fireplace was at the very center of home life, and was used not only for warmth but also for cooking.

Cooking on a fireplace requires a great deal more effort and time than using a stove. Dry kindling is used to start the fire, and green wood is cut and brought in to burn, since seasoned wood burns too quickly and gives off less heat. For cooking, there must be a hot bed of coals—a process that takes a full hour for a new fire to produce. Then, as the coals die down, more wood is added slowly to maintain the temperature.

Some fireplaces had iron bars built from side to side about three feet above the fireplace floor. Others had a bar that was hinged to the side wall of the fireplace so it could be hung with an "S" shaped hook.

People used pots suspended over the fire for heating soups and stews, boiling meat and vegetables, and heating large quantities of water. If the fire got too hot, or if something only needed to be kept warm, the pot could be slid along the bar to the side or swung partly out of the fireplace.

One of the most useful cooking utensils was the Dutch Oven. A true Dutch Oven is a large, heavy, round, cast iron pot, with or without a long handle, and an iron lid with a half-inch lip all the way around the edge. It also has four small legs to keep it suspended over the fire or coals.

The Dutch Oven was used to bake a variety of things that needed baking. It was placed on hot coals to preheat it while the lid was placed directly on the fire. When the oven and lid are hot enough, the biscuits or bread dough were either poured or cut and placed in the slightly-greased oven and the lid set on top with a pair of tongs. Coals were then piled on top of the lid for additional heat. The lip around the edge kept them from rolling off.

One had to be careful that the coals under the oven were not too hot or the food would burn. The lid could be much hotter than the bottom, as it was not directly touching what was being baked.

Your imagination is your best asset in any situation, especially when your survival and the survival of your family depend upon your knowledge and know how.

Two cast iron skillets may be used to bake biscuits or cornbread in the same way you would use a Dutch Oven. Set the larger skillet, filled with hot coals, on top of the small one that has been slightly greased and the batter poured into it. Or, if you have a fireplace, a piece of metal such as tin, galvanized tin, stainless steel, or any metal with a bright shiny surface may be used in the same way to reflect the heat as a reflector oven.

The Wood Stove

Wood stoves are considered to be an improvement over fireplace cooking; however they still require a lot of attention. As with the fireplace, dry kindling and sticks of wood have to be cut to fit the firebox and kept on hand.

The fire is built in the firebox located on the left-hand side of the stove under the cooking surface. The damper in the stove pipe and the vent in the stove are opened all the way until a roaring fire is started. Once the fire has started to burn, the damper and front vent may be adjusted to keep enough oxygen in the firebox to keep the fire burning hot but slowly. (The damper, when closed, seals off the right side of the firebox and greatly cuts the circulation of heat. It does not put the fire out, but cools the rest of the stove so that it can be left unattended fairly safely.)

not put the fire out, but cools the rest of the stove so that it can be left unattended fairly safely).

Once the oven reaches the desired temperature, bread, cakes, and other items may be placed in the oven for baking.

The first few times you try to bake biscuits on a wood cook stove they may be either nicely browned but raw in the center, or burned black. However, you can learn through trial and error how the damper and front vent must be coordinated one with the other. With the addition of a few pieces of wood from time to time, you too can become a gourmet cook.

Chapter Nineteen

Survival Tools

The basic tools for survival on the suggested list below have been chosen both for simplicity and necessity.

First and foremost, your goal is to be as self-sustaining as possible.

Each family must survey their own needs and talents to choose those survival tools which would be appropriate for them.

Tools	Use
Cross cut saw	firewood—or trees for house
Hand saw	construction
Double bladed ax	chop wood
Ax and foot adtx combination	make timbers
Splitting ax	splitting fire wood
Hatchet	splitting kindling
Hammer (claw)	construction
Hammer (saw set)	setting saw
Wedge (iron)	split wood, or cutting trees
Saw set tool	sets saw teeth
Saw gauge	sharpens saw teeth
File (flat)	sharpen tools
File (triangle 6)	file hand saws
Drawing knife	shape building timber
Wood chisel	chisel wood
Pick ax	pick mallet

Shovel	garden
Rake	garden
Hoe	garden
Froe	to split shakes
Well pulley	draw water
200' or more ¾" rope	miscellaneous
Well bucket	carry water

Chapter Twenty

Soap Making

Soap for good and vibrant health is a vital item in any home storage program. Without soap we would not be able to have clean bodies or clean clothes and infection and disease would be prevalent throughout our homes. Therefore, store plenty of soap or the ingredients to make your own.

Here a few simple recipes for soap making. You need plenty of lard or old clean grease (must be animal fat only), lye, a few other ingredients and a large pot for boiling and you have everything necessary to "whomp" up a batch.

Remember, practice makes perfect before an emergency, not after.

Grandmother's Homemade Soap

1 can lye, or quart homemade lye
18 cups warm water
14 cups grease (must be animal fat)
½ cup ammonia
¾ cup borax

Dissolve the lye in water. Let it cool until lukewarm. Melt the grease, and cool it to lukewarm. Add to lye. Add ammonia and borax. Stir until thick. Pour into containers. Let it set a few days, then cut it into bars.

Soap Like Mother Used to Make

Put on a pair of rubber gloves. Prepare a clean iron or enamel container of large size, about three yards of cheese cloth (doubled twice), a wooden spoon for stirring, a large cardboard box, a roll of wax paper (not plastic), a roll of old newspaper, and an old sheet.

Melt 6 pounds of waste animal fat, and strain it through the cheese cloth twice. Over a warm fire: Dissolve a 13-ounce can of lye in 2½ pints of cold water in large enamel container, stirring constantly. Add ½ cup borax and continue stirring until this dissolves. When the solution is warm, trickle grease into it. Continue stirring until the solution thickens to the consistency of cake batter (more than an hour.)

Pour it into a box lined with wax paper and cloth. Put several layers of old newspaper under the box to absorb grease. In 18 to 24 hours the solution should be firm enough to cut into cakes. Turn it out of the box, remove the cloth lining, and allow the cakes to dry two or three days.

Homemade Soap

3 cans lye
10 quarts water
12 pounds lard or old grease (clean). Must be animal fat.
18 quarts water

Mix the lye and ten quarts of water, and bring it to a boil. Add twelve pounds lard or old clean grease and boil it slowly for one hour. Then add eighteen quarts of water and continue cooking. When the mixture is the consistency of heavy syrup, pour it into a mold. Cut into bars when cold.

Laundry Soap

1 can lye   ¾ cup ammonia
½ cup borax   ¾ cup kerosene
5 pounds grease (must be animal fat)

Melt the lye in one quart of water. Dissolve the borax in one cup water and add to lye mixture. Melt grease and add ammonia and kerosene, and then to the lye, then stir until it thickens. Pour it into molds, or use milk cartons. (You could use a grater to make a grated laundry soap.)

A Good Soap

Mix one quart cold water and a one pound can lye in a stone jar (crock) or granite pan. Stir until it cools. Add one tablespoon washing ammonia, two tablespoons 20 Mule Team borax and five pounds of any clean grease, (must be animal fat) warmed until it will run easily. Stir until it thickens. Pour it into molds, cut it into bars before it gets too hard. Wait a few weeks before using.

How to Make Lye

One necessary ingredient for making soap is lye. Without this valuable ingredient soap cannot be made. Since lye can be homemade, here are some instructions on how to make lye out of your fireplace ashes and a diagram to enable you to make a "Lye Hopper".

1. In bottom of a lye hopper or wooden barrel, place some straw about ½" to 1" deep. Be sure to put a cork into hole in the lower front of the hopper.

2. Save all your fireplace ashes and put them in the ash hopper or barrel on top of the straw.

3. Lye can be made from any wood ash, although oak and hickory make the best lye.

4. When the hopper is full of ashes and you are ready to make lye, add water a gallon or two at a time, until the hopper is full of water. Let it set for about 24 hours. Put a bucket under the hole in the lower front of the hopper and carefully pull the plug, letting the lye drip slowly into the bucket.

5. *Caution!!* This liquid is pure *lye* and is *very dangerous* to children. The process is a very slow one and every precaution should be taken to insure the safety of small children.

6. When the bucket is full, the lye is ready to make soap.

A simple recipe for making soap: put the lye in a large pot, bring it to a full boil. Add 10 to 15 lbs. lard. Stir until mixture thickens like syrup. Pour it into molds, then let it set a few days before cutting it.

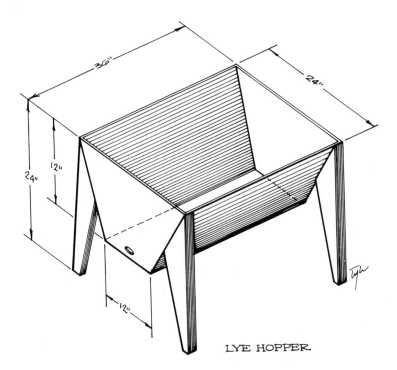

LYE HOPPER

Chapter Twenty-one

Candle Molding

Candle molding can be an exciting adventure for a family needing an outlet for creativity. Almost anything can be used as a mold, nothing fancy has to be purchased. Use your imagination in selecting your molds.

For example, you can use a muffin tin, an empty pop can, a jello mold, a custard cup, a pretty long-stemmed glass, paper cups, milk cartons, empty cardboard paper towel tubes— the list is endless.

The candle described is a versatile one, and should be carried in the trunk of every automobile during the winter months with a book of safety matches. This candle could keep you warm inside your car in case of an emergency breakdown. Or if the need should arise, you could even use it to warm a can of soup or a baby's bottle.

Candle wax in a fifty pound cube may be purchased from hobby shops.

You will need the following equipment and ingredients:

double boiler
measuring cups
newspaper
wire wicking or plain wicking
long handled wooden spoon
several number 10 cans for molds

wax, 8 lbs.
stearine or stearic acid
large dishpan
sawdust, 5 lbs.

Now comes the fun of making one or two survival candles. Take one number ten can (gallon size) and with your imagination divide the can into quarters. Cut the wicking into four nine-inch pieces. Tie two pieces of wicking onto a pencil two inches from each end. Take another pencil and tie the remaining two pieces of wicking the same way, two inches from each end. Anchor the pencils in the shape of a cross over the top of the empty can, then set the can aside.

Fill the large dishpan about half full of sawdust, warm in a moderate oven (200 degrees) for about ten to fifteen minutes.

While the sawdust is warming melt the wax in a double boiler, adding stearine or stearic acid per package directions, mix together until the stearine is well blended and completely dissolved.

When the sawdust is warm, spread newspapers on your work table. Set the dishpan full of sawdust on top of newspapers, immediately drizzle the melted wax on top of sawdust. Working very quickly, mix the two together with a spoon. Ladle the mixture into the number ten can, being careful not to displace the wicking from the pencils. This will give you a large candle with four wicks. You may light all four at once for cooking and extra warmth or you may use one wick at a time.

Let the candle set a few days before using it, to give the wax a chance to harden. Burning time is approximately 52 hours.

A word of warning! Don't pour any leftover melted wax down your sink drain, it will harden immediately. Put all utensils in a warm oven for a few minutes to melt the wax. Be sure and cover the oven rack with foil to catch the melted wax.

Caution! When using a survival candle in a car, trailer, camper or other enclosed area, leave a *window open a crack.* Burning wood emits *Carbon Monoxide,* a colorless, odorless, very toxic gas that can cause death in a tightly-closed place.

Chapter Twenty-two

Shoe Making and Repairing

The complete art of shoe making and repairing is beyond the scope of this book; and is sufficiently specialized that few will wish to learn it. Yet it would be helpful to obtain a few basic tools just in case you must provide for your family's needs in an emergency situation. The basic tools include:

1. Jack—stand for holding lasts
2. Lasts—various sizes, the metal the shoe fits on
3. Tacks—various sizes
4. Hammer—if you can find one
5. Knives—for cutting and trimming leather

If in need of shoes, you can make Indian moccasins or Mexican huaraches. While making moccasins is quite simple, finding buckskin is quite a problem. However, home tanned rawhide may work, providing enough room is allowed for shrinkage. Since moccasins are worn outside they tend to get wet, and when they dry, the leather tends to become hard and stiff. If rubbing them by hand does not soften the leather, rub them with a little mink oil or mink balm. Mink oil is another good storage item for use on all leather goods.

In many countries people with limited income resole their shoes or make sandals using tire treads as the shoe sole.

Chapter Twenty-three

Tanning Hides

The tanning of hides with a few simple hand hewn tools, strong wood ashes, lye soap and water was the only means available to our forefathers for preserving animal skins for many farm uses.

We do not intend to expound in great detail the complicated methods of tanning hides. But there is a simple way of preserving animal skins, should the need arise, without the use of all the chemicals modern technology uses today.

After the animal has been freshly skinned, place ashes from your fireplace, wood cook stove or lye hopper on the hair side of the skin. Wet the ashes with water, being careful not to wash the ashes off the skin. Gather the skin up, or roll it and put it in the tanning mixture. To make a tanning mixture, put one and a half shovelfuls of ashes per gallon of water into a crock, old bathtub, tanning trough, or barrel. Put the skin in the tanning mixture, pushing it all the way down into the container, and making sure the skin is completely covered. Let it set until the hair starts to loosen. Be sure to stir the mixture several times a day. This will assure you the tanning mixture will reach all the folds of the skin.

When the hair starts to loosen, pull all the hair off the skin. Then wash the skin in clear water. With a wooden board made into a scraper, scrape off any remaining hair left on the hide. Be sure to scrape away any excess fat or flesh on the flesh side of the skin. Soak the skin overnight in good soapy water—this will retard the action of the lye, and keep the skin from being ruined.

Now you are ready to store away the tanned hide or to use it to make whatever you wish.

To tan small hides such as rabbit, mink, ermine, and muskrat, first wash the hide with lukewarm soapy water, using a mild soap. Lay the skin on a flat board, hair side down. With a sharp knife carefully scrape all the flesh from the hide. Cover the clean hide with a thick batter of sourdough. When the dough begins to dry, start working the skin. Be prepared; the next step is going to take a lot of work. Rub the skin with a circular motion against the palm of the hand. Rub and knead the skin until it is dry and soft.

Chapter Twenty-four

White Gas and Kerosene

There is extreme danger involved in storing white gas and kerosene; so some knowledge concerning the storage of these items may be helpful to you. If you decide you need to store kerosene or white gas for later cooking and heating, follow these simple instructions carefully. You need not worry about a catastrophe.

1. Store white gas or kerosene in a 55-gallon drum *full* to the *brim*. Leave no room whatsoever for air or expansion.
2. Next, bury the drum in the ground, away from any burning area, place dirt about one or two feet over the top of the drum.
3. Don't forget where you buried your cache of gas. It will stay without breaking down for a number of years.

Regular gasoline for cars can be stored the same way *except* it will last only about one or two years without breaking down.

Chapter Twenty-five

Survival Garden

To be able to grow vegetables from one year to the next, you need good, strong garden seeds for your survival garden.

Care should be taken when selecting your survival seeds. If you select hybrid seeds, they are not good producers for the following year.

You can, if the season permits, harvest your own garden seeds for storage.

There are commercial firms that package seeds especially for storage that are stored in airtight containers with a good variety of survival seeds in them.

Whether you harvest your own or buy them commercially, every storage program should include a good variety of seeds.

Sweeten the Soil

For the best results of growing your own vegetables follow these simple suggestions.

To make your soil productive you must plow your soil about 12 inches deep in the fall and plant a cover crop such as soybeans, cowpeas, rye or red clover. When the crop is fully grown, first drag it down, then plow it under. Make certain you plough it deep. Soybeans replenish the soil with all the vitamins and minerals more rapidly than red clover or any of the other items you may plant. When you plough your cover crop, plough in a criss cross pattern each year. This will thoroughly pulverize the soil and bring the rich unused soil to the surface. Ploughing deep allows the roots of your vegetables to go deep into the ground and draw both water and nourishment.

Water Properly

Most people, in growing their own gardens, never water their vegetables enough. In a hurry they grab the garden hose, sprinkle the tops of the plants once each day for five minutes or so, then go on their way. Later they wonder why their vegetables have shriveled up and died. Vegetable gardens need to be watered with a sprinkler or soaker system to enable the water to penetrate the soil very deeply. Watering doesn't take very long but should be done thoroughly, either before 9:00 a.m. or after 5:00 p.m. Never water your garden in the heat of the day.

After your seeds have started to come up, keep the soil loose to enable the sun, oxygen and other life-giving elements to penetrate. When weeds start to grow in your garden keep them pulled out, as they can choke the life out of your vegetables.

Plant Tomatoes Early

To grow beautiful tomatoes plant the seed early in your greenhouse or a window-box and replant them several times before you plant them in your garden. This makes a stronger plant with larger fruit. If tomatoes don't ripen, or you have a short growing season, pull all but 4 or 5 leaves from the plant. This will enable the sun to reach the fruit and hasten ripening. We have learned to plant tomatoes in a deep trench, about 2 feet deep. We fill the trench 18 inches deep with compost. After filling with compost we fill the rest with soil that has been finely pulverized. In this fine soil we plant our young tomato plants. The soil is fine enough to allow water and sun to soak deep into the soil. The compost is filled with rich vitamins and minerals to enable the plant to grow and produce beautiful healthy fruit with a minimum of water.

What is Compost?

Compost boxes are used with a great deal of success in the Pacific Northwest for growing strong healthy vegetables. To make a compost pile or box, measure a site away from the main house the size you desire, the most common is about 5' x 5'. Scraps such as tablescraps, chicken feathers, cut grass, leaves, chicken and rabbit entrails, watermelon rinds, and so on are put into the compost to deteriorate. Once this is accomplished, everything is mixed and mulched together. The compost is moist and oozing with life-giving properties to make your vegetable garden grow more abundantly than ever before. We feel everyone should learn all about a compost pile or box. It is truly useful in growing large, plump, mouthwatering fruit or vegetables.

Part 6
Diversified Food Preparation

Chapter Twenty-six

Cookies and Crackers

To teach the homemaker how important it is to the health of her family for her to become fully acquainted with wheat and all its uses has been a very difficult task. Most homemakers, when trying new foods, are afraid of the loss of valuable ingredients. No one wants to lose precious grocery items. With inflation increasing every year, only a limited number have the financial resources to experiment with new recipes.

If we could prove the "storing what you use and use what you store" approach could save as much as twenty-five percent of your annual food budget, would you try it? Of course you would. We are going to teach you how to do exactly that, provided you incorporate wheat in your daily menus. For the time being, use it weekly, then slowly increase to daily usage.

The recipes we are going to give you now cost no more than 25 to 35 cents per recipe. (Except for graham crackers, one recipe makes 3½ pounds at 29 cents per pound.)

Graham Crackers

1 cup oil
1 cup raw or brown sugar
½ cup honey
2 eggs

½ cup evaporated milk
2 tsp. lemon or vinegar
2 tsp. vanilla
6 cups whole wheat flour*

*Add 1 tsp. salt and 2 tsp. baking soda to one cup

Mix together: evaporated milk and lemon juice. Add oil, honey, vanilla, eggs, and sugar. Add all ingredients to flour and mix. Divide into four equal parts. Place on greased and floured cookie sheet. Roll to edges with bottle or pizza roller ¼" thick. Bake at 375 degrees for twenty minutes or until brown. Cut into squares immediately when taken from the oven. Makes three and a half pounds at 29 cents per pound.

Whole Wheat Snack Crackers

2 cups whole wheat flour
2½ tsp. seasoned vegetable salt
5 tbsp. oil
¾ cup water

Combine flour and salt. Add oil and mix thoroughly. Stir in water, mixing well. Roll very thin on floured board. Sprinkle with sesame seeds, rolling seeds in lightly. Bake at 425 degrees for 8-10 minutes.

Whole Wheat Sesame Thins

1 cup whole wheat flour   ½ tsp. salt
¼ cup soya flour   sesame seeds
¼ cup wheat germ   3 tbsp. oil

Mix well with 6 tbsp. water. Form into a firm ball and roll very thin on floured board. Sprinkle generously with sesame seeds. Roll seeds into dough well. Score dough in a diagonal pattern (for diamond shaped crackers) with a knife or pastry wheel. Lift to baking sheet. Bake at 425 degrees for 10-12 minutes or until brown. Separate crackers after baking.

Honey Drop Cookies

½ cup ground sprouted wheat
1 cup wheat flour
½ cup water
1½ tbsp. dry milk
⅓ cup honey, or more
½ tsp. vanilla

Mix well, drop teaspoonfuls of mixture onto a greased cookie sheet. Flatten with the back of a spoon. Bake 20 minutes at 350 degrees.

These simple wheat recipes with so few ingredients, and little monetary involvement, are made to order for the "just learning" homemaker.

With success behind you, you will be inspired to try more complex wheat cookery for the health of your family and the savings in your budget.

Chapter Twenty-seven

Breads and Cereals

Absolutely nothing smells better than the aroma of freshly-baked homemade bread. Spreading it with butter and honey is a real taste treat.

Many homemakers have once again resumed the creative art of breadmaking, due to the ever-increasing price of store-bought or commercially prepared baked goods.

Few realize there is more to be saved by using freshly ground whole wheat flour than by purchasing enriched white flour. Not only are the savings worthwhile, but there also is a substantial increase in the nutritional value of baked goods.

One hundred percent whole wheat bread is very difficult to make by hand. However, if you follow these instructions, you should be able to make a light, plump loaf of whole wheat bread.

First, don't cheat—don't fudge by using a mixture of fifty percent white flour. White flour will automatically lighten the loaf. Try this recipe.

Never Fail Whole Wheat Bread

1. Sprinkle:
   2 tbsp. yeast in
   ½ cup warm water (do not stir)

2. Mix well in order given
   5 cups hot water from tap
   ⅔ cup honey
   ⅔ cup cooking oil
   1 tbsp. salt
   7 cups unsifted whole wheat flour
3. Add:
   Yeast
   5 or 6 cups whole wheat flour
4. Stir.
5. Pour ¼ of the dough at a time in a nest of flour. Combine the flour balls and knead well for 5-10 minutes. (At this point, I would suggest the use of a rubber mallet to beat the dough for 10 minutes—15 minutes is much better.) It is an absolute must to develop the gluten, otherwise the loaf will be coarse and heavy. Oil may be used on the hands and board.
6. Divide into 6 sections or portions according to pan sizes. Shape into loaves and put in lightly oiled pans. Let rise until dough is ⅓ higher than when first put in the pan. Bake at 350 degrees for about forty minutes. Brush tops with butter and remove from pans.

Quick Wheat Bread

3 cups warm water
3 pkgs. dry yeast
⅓ cup honey
⅓ cup oil

6-6½ cups whole wheat
   flour, unsifted
1 tbsp. salt
1 cup powdered milk

Mix water, yeast, honey, and oil. Sift dry ingredients together and add to first mixture. Let stand in warm place for 15 minutes. Knead well for 10 minutes. Form into loaves and place in two well-greased loaf pans. Let rise 15 minutes in warm oven, 80-85 degrees. Remove bread and heat oven to 350-375 degrees. Replace in oven and bake 50-55 minutes. Brush tops with butter.

Roll Dough
(will keep 3-4 days in refrigerator)

Soften 2 packages yeast in ½ cup warm water. Set aside and let it stand 5 minutes.

Combine:
> 1 cup scalded milk
> ½ cup sugar
> 3 tsp. salt
> ½ cup shortening

Add 1 cup water. Cool to lukewarm. Add softened yeast. Sift and measure 9 cups flour. Work in half of the sifted flour, beat for 1 minute. Add 2 eggs, blend thoroughly, work in remaining flour. Turn dough onto lightly floured board, shape into round ball. Cover with towel, let rest 10 minutes. Knead 5 minutes. Dough is ready for use.

If you wish to store, place in greased bowl, grease dough top lightly, and cover with piece of plastic or 2 layers of waxed paper. Tie securely and chill. Punch dough down occasionally when necessary.

Quick Boston Brown Bread

In large bowl sift:
> 3½ cups flour
> 2¾ cup Kellogg All Bran Cereal Mix
> 1 tsp. salt

In another large bowl beat:
> 1 egg
> ¾ cup sugar
> 1 cup molasses
> 2 cups sour milk or buttermilk

Dissolve 2 teaspoons of baking soda in milk before adding to rest of mixture. Turn into bowl of dry ingredients and mix well. Fill 5 medium size vegetable cans ½ full and bake 1½ hours at 325 degrees.

Whole Wheat Batter Bread

Measure into large mixing bowl:
> 2½ cups warm water
> 2 pkg. dry yeast, stir to dissolve

Mix in another large bowl:
    2 cups unsifted whole wheat flour
    4 cups sifted unbleached flour
    4 tsp. salt
Add ½ of the flour mixture and:
    ¼ cup soft shortening
    ¼ cup honey or brown sugar

Beat on medium 2 minutes. Add remaining flour mixture and blend with spoon until smooth. Scrape down batter, cover with paper in bowl, and let rise until double (30 min.) Stir down batter by beating 25 strokes. Divide batter in 2 greased loaf pans. Let rise to top of pans (40 min.) Bake at 375 degrees for 40-50 minutes.

Cracked Wheat Bread

¼ cup cracked wheat
1 cup cold water
¼ tsp. salt

Bring to a boil. Then simmer 20 minutes. When cool add to:

½ cup milk   1 ¼ tsp. salt
1 ½ tbsp. shortening   1 pkg. dry yeast (dissolved
1 tbsp. sugar   in 1 cup water)
1 cup water   2 tsp. light molasses

Add approximately 3 cups of sifted flour to make stiff dough.
Let rise until double in bulk—until it recedes to light touch. Punch down, then let rise to about ¾ of its former size. Make in loaf size. Round up and let rise 20 minutes. Form into loaves and let rise until double in bulk. Bake thoroughly at 400 degrees.

Everlasting Yeast

Every homemaker ought to have on hand an everlasting yeast recipe or, better yet, a jar of everlasting yeast in her cupboard. The bread made from this yeast is light in texture, has a light yeasty smell and is delicious.

Everlasting yeast differs slightly from sourdough. It must be fed every thirty days even if it has not been used for making bread. Sourdough starter, on the other hand, need not be fed. Kept cool, it will last for years.

1 cake yeast
½ cup sugar

1 pint lukewarm potato water

Dissolve yeast in 1 pint potato water, mix well. Add ½ cup sugar and stir thoroughly. Pour into a 2-quart glass jar; cover loosely and let stand in a warm place overnight. In the morning, put lid on jar and screw cover tight. Set away in a cool place. When ready to make bread, pour one pint potato water into the yeast. Mix well; then stir in ¼ cup sugar or honey. Let stand in warm place for 5 hours or overnight; then stir it down and use one pint of the mixture for making four loaves of bread. Cover the rest and keep in cool place.

Bread Made with Everlasting Yeast

2 cups milk
⅓ cup shortening
1 ½ tbsp. salt

1 pint everlasting yeast
12-14 cups flour

Scald milk and cool until lukewarm. Add yeast, shortening and 4 cups flour. Beat vigorously 1-2 minutes; cover and allow to rise ½ hour. Then add salt and rest of flour. Knead until elastic to touch; cover and let rise until double in bulk. Shape into loaves and again let rise until doubled. Brush with milk and bake about 1 hour at 400 degrees. For a golden brown crust, add a tablespoon or two of milk to beaten egg.

Here are some more economy recipes to help you learn the different uses of wheat. Cereal is the backbone of many a homemaker's menus for breakfast for her family. The recipes here are both simple and inexpensive, to once again show a real saving in your grocery budget.

Homemade Cream of Wheat

Grind about 4 cups wheat on the setting of your wheat mill for wheat grits (medium, or maybe slightly toward fine). Do not sift. Measure 4 cups water and ½ tsp. salt, then bring to boil. Slowly add ½ cup cream of wheat that has been mixed with ¼ to ½ cup water. Stir vigorously until well blended to keep mixture from lumping. Makes 6 four-ounce servings. Cost about 2 cents per serving.

Whole Wheat Cereal

1 cup whole grain wheat
4 cups water
1 tsp. salt

The night before, add wheat to salted, boiling water. Boil for about 10 minutes, cover and let stand on pilot overnight. Wheat will be ready to eat by morning. Serve with warm milk, sugar, or honey and butter.

Whole Wheat Flake Cereal

1 cup whole wheat flour   1 cup milk
¼ tsp. salt   honey to taste

Mix together into a thin batter. Pour onto a lightly greased cookie sheet (with rim), about 1/8 inch deep. Bake at 375 degrees for about 15-20 minutes, or until lightly brown. Remove from pan, let cool, then break into small pieces. Store in a jar with a tight-fitting lid. To serve, pour into bowl, add milk. Makes about 12-16 servings.

Helen's Granola

There is nothing as adaptable as Granola. So use what you have on hand, mix, match, add a lot, take away a little until you have the right combination to satisfy your taste buds.

4-6 cups oatmeal   ½ cup raisins
¼-½ cup honey   ½ cup dates
1 cup sesame seeds   1 cup chopped nuts
1 cup soy grits

Pour oatmeal in 9" x 13" flat pan. Place in oven at 200-400 degrees. Stir every two or three minutes and toast until golden brown.

When oats are golden, remove from oven and quickly drizzle honey over oats until all is gone. Quickly mix together, adding other ingredients as you mix and blend. Store in tightly closed container until ready to use. Makes about 10 four-ounce servings.

Chapter Twenty-eight

Main Dishes

Using wheat with other ingredients to make a main dish is another way to become accustomed to wheat in your diet. These dishes are nourishing, economical and very palatable. Even the most inexperienced cook will be able to create meals that will be worthy of applause from her family.

Of all the different foods that can be made with wheat, gluten is by far the most versatile. As an entree you can accomplish the effect you desire by adding a little spice or even baking, grinding, cubing, to make steaks.

On the market today there are three well written volumes covering the subject of gluten. See *Creative Wheat Cookery,* by Evelyn Ethington, or refer to Esther Dickey's *Passport To Survival* or to *The Gluten Book* by LeArta Moulton.

Whole Wheat Salad

1 cup mayonnaise
1 cup chopped onion
6 cups cooked whole wheat
   (boiled, or steamed about 1
   hour)
4 tbsp. finely chopped green pepper

½ tsp. salt
1 cup sea food
Seasoned salt, seasoned
   pepper, and garlic may
   be added.

Mix and let stand several hours. For a real taste treat, add smoked fish.

Steamed Whole Wheat

1 cup whole wheat
1 tsp. salt
2 cups water

Put the water in double boiler, add wheat and salt, cook till tender. Serve like rice as a side dish, or vegetable with gravy.

Gluten Casserole

Brown 3 cups ground gluten with one large chopped onion. Add ½ cup bell pepper, one can mushroom soup, one can fresh milk. Blend together, pour into buttered one quart casserole dish. Sprinkle top with grated cheese and chopped parsley. Bake about 30 minutes in moderate oven, 350 degrees. Serves six.

Gluten Stew

Dredge four cups gluten cubes in seasoned flour. Brown in 2 or 3 tbsp. oil, pour into large stew pot with about one quart of water, add more if needed. Bring to a boil, turn heat to simmer, and simmer for about 30 minutes. Add salt, pepper, garlic, and other seasonings to taste. Add prepared vegetables, potatoes, carrots, celery, and onions. Turn heat to high, after bringing up to a boil, turn to medium. Thicken with cornstarch, if necessary.

Basic Soybean Recipe

1 cup dry soybeans
⅔ cup tomato juice
½ cup flour
1 tsp. salt or to taste

1 medium onion
½ cup peanut butter
1 tbsp. oil

Soak beans overnight. Drain and wash the beans. Run beans and onions through a food grinder using finest blade. A blender may be used, but the results in texture will be different. Add remaining ingredients. Place in cans or jars and cover. Steam 3 hours in a boiling water bath. The water should come halfway up on the cans, and the lids should be tight. Or you may use a pressure cooker, cooking at 10 pounds pressure for 1½ hours. You may choose to make a large batch while you are at it, and put it in 1 pint canning jars, filling them to about 1 inch from the top. Then put on lids and rings and process in the pressure cooker. The beans cook, the jars seal, and you have enough preserved in the jars for several months. You may find the half-pint wide-mouth jars handy when making lunches. Add a little chopped pickle, celery, bell pepper, black olives, egg, and mayonnaise. Or you may try this: Make an open faced sandwich, top with cheese and brown under the broiler.

Vary the amount of tomato juice or the amount of flour and you will get a drier or stiffer product. Omitting peanut butter makes it crumble easily. Use mayonnaise for sandwich binders or egg for patties.

Soybean Patties

1 cup cooked rice	2 tbsp. chopped onion
2 eggs	½ tsp. salt
½ tsp. celery salt	
2 cups cooked soybeans, mashed	
1 cup soft whole wheat bread crumbs	

Mix all ingredients together. Form into patties and bake at 350 degrees until brown, about 45 minutes. Serves six. Just before serving, spoon cheese sauce over tops of patties.

Soybean Loaf

1 cup dried soybeans	3 cups vegetable broth
4 tbsp. vegetable oil	2 tbsp. molasses
1 medium onion, chopped	¼ tsp. powdered kelp
juice of ½ lemon	

Pour 3 cups of hot broth over washed beans and soak for 24 to 36 hours. Put on to boil in the same broth and keep beans covered until they develop a light tan color. Transfer to a covered baking dish and add oil and molasses. Bake in a slow oven until beans are browned and well done. Stir occasionally during baking and keep beans in liquid until the last ½ hour. Add onion, kelp and lemon juice and bake uncovered for the last half hour to allow the top to brown.

Soybean Casserole

2 cups cooked drained soybeans   2 tbsp. peanut or soy oil
½ cup coarsely chopped onion   ½ tsp. minced garlic
½ lb. lean sausage   salt and pepper
¼ cup coarsely chopped green pepper
½ cup grated sharp cheddar cheese

In a skillet, saute the onion, green pepper and garlic in the oil until vegetables start to brown. Crumble in the sausage meat and continue to cook until it is rather well browned, stirring often. Pour off excess fat. Add the soybeans, season to taste and mix thoroughly. Pour into a one-quart casserole. Sprinkle with cheese and bake in preheated oven at 350 degrees for 20 minutes or until cheese has melted and is lightly browned.

Recipes Using Textured Vegetable [Soy] Protein [T.V.P.]

Lasagna

1 cup T.V.P. or T.S.P.   1 cup hot water
1-8 oz. can tomato sauce   1-1lb. 13 oz. can tomatoes
½ tsp. garlic powder   1 pkg. spaghetti sauce mix
1 pkg. lasagna noodles   ½ cup Parmesan cheese
8 oz. Mozzarella cheese, sliced
1 pint Ricotta cheese, well drained (Cottage cheese may be
    substituted for the Ricotta)

Add hot water to T.V.P. and let set for about 15 minutes. In dutch oven, combine tomatoes, tomato sauce, garlic powder and spaghetti sauce mix. Add T.V.P. and mix thoroughly. Cover and simmer 30 minutes. Meanwhile, boil lasagna in salted water till almost tender, drain and rinse. Pour ¼ of the sauce into 11 x 7 x 2 inch baking dish. Cover sauce with ⅓ of the noodles. Add Mozzarella slices and then a layer of Ricotta cheese. Repeat layers ending with sauce and top with Parmesan cheese. Casserole may be refrigerated overnight, frozen or baked. Bake at 350 degrees for 30 minutes. Remove from oven and allow to set for 10 minutes before serving. Serves 6-8.

Taco Buns

1 cup T.V.P.
½ cup chopped onion
1 8 oz. can tomato sauce
1 cup crushed corn chips
2 cups shredded lettuce
3 oz. American cheese, shredded
mayonnaise

¾ cup hot water
3 tbsp. oil
1 /8 tsp. garlic powder
8 hamburger buns
1 cup diced tomatoes

Rehydrate T.V.P. in hot water for 10 minutes. Saute onions in oil. Add rehydrated T.V.P., tomato sauce and garlic powder. Mix well. Simmer 5 minutes. Stir in crushed corn chips. Spoon mixture on toasted bun. Top with tomato, lettuce and cheese. Spread mayonnaise on top half. Place top on bottom as if it were a sandwich. Serves 8.

Salted Soybeans

Salted soys are prized for their rich nutty flavor. Because soybeans contain so much protein and fat, they are good fried in deep fat and salted and served like salted nuts. Wash and soak dry soybeans overnight, then drain and spread them out at room temperature until surface is dry. Fry a few at a time in deep fat (350 degrees) for 10 minutes. Drain on absorbent paper and sprinkle with salt while still warm.

Parched Mixed Grains

In a frying pan (no oil), put just enough wheat, rice, soybeans, pumpkin, etc. to cover the bottom. Shake pan over high heat until the crackling sounds very minimum. You may open the lid to watch so that the grain or seeds do not get too brown. Do only one type of grain or seed at a time and combine them after they are parched. Add oil, salt, vegetable seasoning or soy sauce.

Suggested combinations: wheat, rice, sunflower seeds, pumpkin seeds, and sesame seeds. Some like to add raisins, and this combination makes a nice party mix.

Chapter Twenty-nine

Desserts

Wheat as a meat substitute? Wheat as a main dish? Wheat for bread and cereals? And now wheat for desserts?

Incredible! Impossible! No! It can be done. Try this cake for a tasty treat made with lots of eggs, sugar and whole wheat flour for a gourmet's delight.

Prize Sponge Cake

6 eggs, separated
1½ cups raw sugar
½ cup water
½ tsp. vanilla
½ tsp. lemon juice or
   lemon extract

¼ tsp. almond extract
1½ cups sifted whole
   wheat flour
½ tsp. salt
1 tsp. cream of tartar

Beat with mixer, yolks, water, sugar, and flavoring for 5 to 7 minutes using small mixing bowl, then transfer to a larger bowl. Mixture will be very thick and creamy. Sift flour and salt together twice. Add to above mixture gradually, continue to beat. Beat egg whites and cream of tartar together until stiff. Do not allow whites to stand, but fold immediately into first mixture. Bake in ungreased angel food pan for one hour to one hour and ten minutes (or until top springs back when lightly touched) at 325 to 350 degrees F. Invert pan and cool thoroughly before removing.

Plain Whole Wheat Cake

½ cup butter or margarine
1½ cups raw or brown sugar
2 tsp. vanilla
1 cup water

2 cups sifted whole
  wheat flour
3 tsp. baking powder
½ cup powdered milk

Cream butter or margarine and sugar. Add egg yolks, one at a time, beating well after each addition. Sift dry ingredients together twice and add alternately with water. Fold in beaten egg whites last. Bake in well greased 9" x 13" pan at 350 degrees for 30 to 35 minutes. Frost or serve with your favorite sauce or topping.

Note: To make a lighter cake made with whole wheat flour, use water instead of milk. If the extra nutritional value of milk is desired, use dry powdered milk by sifting ¼ to ½ cup of dry milk powder with other dry ingredients, and use water in place of the liquid milk called for.

Easy Flaky Pie Crust

2 cups sifted whole wheat flour
¾ cup shortening or butter
½ tsp. salt

¼ cup flour
5 to 10 tsp. water

Sift flour and salt together. Cut in shortening or butter with pastry blender, or two table knives, until pieces are the size of small peas. Mix the ¼ cup flour and 5 to 10 tsp. water together (mix water, a spoonful at a time after the first, with the ¼ cup flour) until the mixture is of medium consistency. Add to the dry ingredients, stirring until well mixed. Pour onto a floured board, divide dough in two pieces, and roll each one into a ball. Take one ball of dough, flatten with hand, then roll with a rolling pin from center to outer edge until 1/8 inch thick. Repeat. Makes two nine inch pie crusts. Bake at 450 degrees for 10 to 12 minutes, or until golden.

Kwik Krazy Kake

1½ cups sifted regular
  all-purpose flour

1 tsp. baking soda
½ tsp. salt

1 tsp. cinnamon
1 cup sugar
¼ cup cocoa
½ cup whole bran cereal

1 cup cold, strong coffee or
Postum
¼ cup vegetable oil
1 tbsp. vinegar
1 tsp. vanilla flavoring

Sift together flour, soda, salt, cinnamon, sugar and cocoa. Set aside. Measure whole bran cereal and coffee or Postum into greased 8 x 8 x 2 inch baking pan; stir to combine. Let stand 1 to 2 minutes or until most of liquid is absorbed. Mix in oil, vinegar and vanilla. Add sifted dry ingredients; stir until smooth.

Bake in moderate oven (350 degrees) about 40 minutes or until a wooden toothpick inserted near the center comes out clean.

Serve with cinnamon flavored whipped topping, orange sauce or ice cream. Sprinkle with nuts, if desired.

Quick Cake

1 egg
2 to 3 tbsp. shortening
milk

1 cup sugar
1¾ cups flour
2 tsp. baking powder

Break the egg in a cup; add the shortening and fill the cup with milk. Pour into a mixing bowl; add the dry ingredients. When all ingredients have been added, beat thoroughly. Pour into well-greased cake pan. The egg may be omitted or 2 egg whites used.

Spread over the top of the cake batter a mixture of ½ cup brown sugar, ½ cup white sugar and 1/8 tsp. salt. Over all pour 1 cup boiling water and place in a moderate oven to bake 1 hour.

If a chocolate sauce is desired, mix 2 tbsp. cocoa with the topping.

Pumpkin Cake

2¼ cups whole wheat pastry flour
3 tsp. baking powder
½ tsp. salt
¼ tsp. baking soda

1½ tsp. cinnamon
½ tsp. ginger
½ tsp. all spice
½ cup shortening

1 cup brown sugar
½ cup sugar
1 egg and 2 yolks

¾ cup buttermilk
¾ can pumpkin
½ cup chopped walnuts

Cream shortening, brown sugar and sugar. Add eggs, buttermilk and pumpkin; mix well. Add dry ingredients; mix well. Pour into well greased pan. Bake at 350 degrees for 35 to 45 minutes. Let stand for 10 minutes and remove from pan.

Sourdough Chocolate Cake

½ cup starter
1 cup milk

1½ cups flour

Mix and let stand 2 or 3 hours in a warm place until bubbly and there is a clean sour milk odor. Or overnight.

2 eggs
½ cup shortening
1 tsp. vanilla

1½ tsp. soda
1 cup sugar
1 tsp. cinnamon
3 squares melted chocolate

Cream shortening, sugar, flavorings, salt and soda. Add eggs one at a time, beating well after each addition. Combine creamed mixture and melted chocolate with sourdough mixture. Stir 300 strokes or mix at a low speed until blended. Pour into two layer pans or one large pan and bake at 350 degrees for 25 minutes or until done. Cool and frost with frosting of your choice. This recipe makes a large 10-inch layer.

Sourdough Starter

2 cups flour
2 cups warm water

1 pkg. dry yeast

Make this starter only when you have forgotten to save a start or when you are making it for the first time. Combine ingredients and mix well. Place in a warm place or closed cupboard overnight. In the morning put ½ cup of the starter in a scalded pint jar with a tight lid and store in the refrigerator or a cool place for future use. This is sourdough starter. The remaining batter can be used immediately for pancakes, waffles, muffins, bread or cake. To increase starter, mix together 2 cups milk, 2 cups flour and ½ cup starter from the jar. Mix together and let set for 6 hours or overnight. Again you are ready to make bread, etc. Remember to save ½ cup of starter for future use.

Honey Cake

1 cup flour	shredded almonds
1 tsp. ground ginger	1 tsp. all spice
4 tbsp. butter or margarine	½ tsp. baking soda
1 egg, beaten	1 cup honey
	½ cup milk

Sift flour, ginger and all spice together. Dissolve baking soda in milk which should be slightly warm. Put butter and honey in bowl over hot water until butter melts. Add beaten egg. Stir in the sifted flour then the milk. Mix thoroughly. Pour into greased 9 x 5 loaf pan. Sprinkle with almonds. Bake at 350 degrees for 30 minutes or until done.

Apple Cheese Loaf

1 cup honey	2 cups sifted flour
½ cup shortening	1 tsp. salt
2 eggs	1½ tsp. baking soda
½ cup grated cheese	1 cup thinly sliced apples
	2 tbsp. apple juice or milk

Using medium speed on mixer, slowly add honey to shortening that has been premeasured into blender. Cream until mixture is light and fluffy. Add eggs and cheese. Blend well. Sift dry ingredients together and fold into batter alternately with apple slices and juice. Mix only until dry ingredients are moistened. Spoon batter into greased 9 x 5 x 3 inch loaf pan. Let stand 15 minutes. Bake at 350 degrees for 60 to 75 minutes. Makes 1 loaf.

Dehydrated apples make excellent desserts.

Honey Raisin Pudding

¾ cup raisins
½ cup honey
4 cups whole wheat bread cubes
1 quart milk

5 eggs
¼ cup sugar
½ tsp. salt
2 tsp. vanilla
2 tsp. nutmeg

Rinse raisins and drain. Combine honey and bread cubes. Cook over low heat and stir until bread absorbs honey (2 to 3 min.). Blend milk, slightly beaten eggs, sugar, salt and vanilla together. Add with raisins to bread cubes. Mix well. Pour into baking dish. Sprinkle with nutmeg. Place dish in pan of hot water and bake at 350 degrees for 1 hour.

Brown Pudding

2 tbsp. butter
2 tsp vanilla
2 tsp. baking powder
1 cup raisins (optional)
1 ½ tsp. soda

½ tsp. salt
1 cup white vinegar
1 tsp. nutmeg
2 cups flour
1 cup milk
1 ½ cups chopped nuts

Combine all ingredients. Pour into baking dish. Combine 2 cups brown sugar, 4 tbsp. butter. Pour over batter. Top with 4 cups boiling water. Bake 40 minutes at 350 degrees.

Part 7

Tips
on
Techniques

Chapter Thirty

Sprout Your Grain

Learning to sprout your seeds and grains is a vital function of your Home Storage and Production Program. Both the economy and nutritional value of sprouted seeds and grains is an asset to your year's supply. Once a seed is sprouted it becomes alive, and in this stage or cycle, the nutritive content is three times that of the unsprouted seed or grain. Research shows that sprouts are among the highest in natural vitamin content per serving of any food obtainable. A handful of seeds costing only a few cents can sprout enough food to provide balanced nutrition for a whole week! With today's rising food costs and deterioration of the quality of our food and our environment, this is truly a viable alternative. No matter who you are or where you live, you can grow your own sprouts and greens in water and a little fertile soil right on your window sill. You can begin right now to produce the food which will nourish your body effectively.

Deficient Soil

The Department of Agriculture is becoming concerned about food deficiencies produced by poor soil. Continuous chemical fertilization prevents plants from receiving all the natural elements they need. When plant life becomes imbalanced, this imbalance is passed on to the people and animals who eat these plants, thus contributing to their malnutrition.

Poor nutrition will eventually lead to overweight and other health problems.

The Chemistry of Seed

In Genesis, God says: "Behold, I have given you every herb bearing seed, which is upon the face of all the earth, and every tree, in which is the fruit of a tree yielding seed; to you it shall be for meat." Luthor Burbank, the great plant wizard, realized the significant values which seeds contain, calling them "natural whole." He was very conscious that the total food values were there. Indeed, the seed is life itself. It contains the vital nourishment our bodies need. A seed is the crucible wherein the alchemy of life works its magic. This tiny space contains the condensed germinating energy, the life-giving elements, the tremendous forces that even scientists do not fully understand. These forces lie dormant in the seed until combined with water, air and sunshine. Then the embryo seed's potential bursts from its shell and life begins!

Sunflower Seed

The sunflower seed is a rich source of vitamins D, B6, B12 and all the essential amino acids. The protein is highly concentrated. Use no more than two ounces a day. Seeds are best eaten after being soaked overnight. Growing them in soil for seven days to produce young greens increases the enzyme content manyfold, converts the fat to carbohydrates and transforms the complex protein into easily digested form.

Sesame Seed

Queen of the oil-bearing seeds, sesame is superior to many seeds because of its high content of calcium and, especially, methionine (a crystalline sulfur containing essential sulphur acids). It is the staple food of the Mediterranean area, and is easy to use raw as a butter, sauce, soup, cheese or milk. In its unhulled form, it contains more calcium than cow's milk; one-and-a-half times more iron than beef liver; three times more phosphorous than eggs; more protein than chicken, beef liver, or beef steak; and more niacin than whole wheat bread.

The phosphorous contained in the seeds is a mineral vital for proper development and maintenance of the bones and teeth. It is especially important for babies and children. Phosphorous also plays a very important part in keeping the brain tissues healthy and alert. Other good sources of phosphorous are whole wheat and oats.

Magnesium, another vital mineral, is scarce in most of our foods. It is essential to the normal functioning of the blood stream and the kidneys. Hair, to be healthy, must have magnesium and vitamin F. Magnesium is available in large amounts in corn, rice, cashew nuts, and wheat.

Alfalfa

How can we use this wonderful plant which contains so many important minerals and vitamins? Simply sprout its seed! These sprouts are especially good when left in sunlight for a day or so to develop tiny leaves of green chlorophyll.

Alfalfa sprouts, after seven days of growth, are an excellent source of chlorophyll. Like all sprouts, they are a rich source of vitamins A, B-complex, and C. They can also provide you with vitamins D, E, G, K and U. The roots of alfalfa extend up to 100 feet into the earth, gathering a wide range of minerals when planted outdoors. Dr. Sherman Davis of the University of Indiana has pointed out that alfalfa is especially rich in iron, calcium, and phosphorous. Dr. Edward Mellenby of England reports that "alfalfa is essential to rebuild decayed teeth." Sprouts are the ideal diet for health, youth, and longevity.

Legumes [including peanuts]

Legumes of every kind are hard to digest and assimilate for most people because of their high concentration of protein and starch and low moisture content. Sprouting transforms them into high quality nourishment.

Mung Beans

After three days of growth, mung bean sprouts become like fruits and vegetables in many ways. According to USDA

Handbook No. 8, *Composition of Foods,* we can make the following observations about mung sprouts: The moisture of the seed increases from 10.7 percent to 88.8 percent in the sprout, comparable to any fruit. The protein becomes less concentrated and more digestible. The germination process converts starch to simple sugars. The carbohydrate content is the same as in casaba melon. The caloric value is slightly less than that of papaya, and a little more than that of honeydew melon. One cup, or ¼ pound, contains 40 calories. Sprouted mung beans have the vitamin A value of a lemon, the thiamin of an avacado, riboflavin of a dried apple, niacin of a banana, and ascorbic acid of a pineapple.

Other legumes suitable for sprouting are lentils, green peas, chick peas and soybeans. Try them all and find your favorites.

Grains

Wheat

Wheat is a staple food all over the world. In sprouted form, wheat becomes an acceptable food. Much of the starch is converted to simple sugars. The vitamin E content triples. Vitamin C is increased by a factor of 6. In the vitamin B complex, the individual vitamin increases range from 20 to 200 percent.

Another good way to use sprouted wheat is to grow the whole wheat berries as a grass. The solid content of juice made from this grass is 70 percent chlorophyll. The enzyme content in chlorophyll, like most whole foods, is rich in laetril (vitamin B-17) which can selectively destroy cancer cells, but has little effect on normal cells. According to Dr. Krebs, the laetril content in sprouts and young fresh greens increases up to 100 times beyond that of the seed from which they originate.

Wheat is a very versatile grain. When sprouted it may be served in salads and many other dishes, or even baked in bread.

Buckwheat

Buckwheat has been largely ignored as food in America. This is unfortunate, as buckwheat is rich in rutin which is necessary for maintaining a healthy bloodstream. Rutin builds up capillaries in the body, preventing hemorrhages. Buckwheat is an aid to persons with high blood pressure and has a cleansing effect on the bloodstream. When used as greens, it provides a high dosage of lecithin.

Barley

Barley was popular in the diet of the Chinese fully twenty centuries before the birth of Christ. An important staple food, it provides many nutrients.

Indoor Greens

These greens are grown on one inch of soil and are ready to eat in seven days: sproutable wheat, unhulled buckwheat, unhulled sunflower, radish or fenugreek seed. Soak each large seed 15 hours; the other small seeds 5 hours. Fill a baking tray or any other flat pan with dark soil. Fifty percent peat moss will make the soil more porous. Mix in a tablespoon of kelp fertilizer (optional). Moisten the soil, but leave no puddles. Spread the seeds next to each other. Cover with wheat paper and a plastic sheet. Put in a warm place. After three days, remove the cover. Place the tray in the light. Water as needed. After four additional days, it is ready to eat—an economical source of chlorophyll year-round.

Buckwheat and Sunflower

Remove any remaining husks and use as salad greens, or juice them. They are rich in amino acids, enzymes, vitamins, chlorophyll. They are low in fat and free from starch.

Fenugreek and Radish

These tangy seasonings for exotic sprout salads are strong liver cleaners.

Wheatgrass

Chew on it, sucking in the juice and spitting out the pulp. If you have a special juicer, you may extract ten ounces of juice from one pound of grass. This requires ¼ pound of seed in planting. Cut it fine for salads, or a blended preparation of it may be added to all cooked foods. A complete food, wheatgrass is high in chlorophyll, which is a good body and blood builder.

Become a Sproutarian

Are you discouraged with the price you pay for your fruits and vegetables? Are you dissatisfied with their poor quality? Why not become a sproutarian? Go to the supermarket today! Get yourself a pound of lentils, soak ½ cup of them in a deep dish in two cups of water for 15 hours. Rinse and drain in the morning and evening for two days. You will have sprouts to put in your salads, to sprinkle on your soups, or to eat plain or with delicious sunflower sourcream.

Almost any seed, grain or legume can be sprouted, although some are tastier than others. You may try mung beans, alfalfa, wheat, peas, fenugreek, chickpeas, radish, fennel, celery seed, etc. These are most readily found in natural food stores. Remember to soak small seeds only 5 hours, beans for 15 hours. You can also mix these seeds. Get a two quart wide mouth jar and a piece of cheesecloth or old nylon stocking, fastened as a cover with a rubber band. Put seeds into the jar as follows: 3 tablespoons of alfalfa, 2 tablespoons of radish or fenugreek, ¼ cup lentils, ½ cup mung beans. Soak these seeds for 15 hours and drain the water. Afterward, rinse and drain well twice daily for three to five days. If you wish to make larger amounts of sprouts so you may share with others, place two cups of mixed seed into a large procelain pot, in the bottom of which holes have been drilled for easy rinsing. Simply place the pot underneath the faucet and rinse morning and evening with warm water. Cover with a plate. The seeds grow beautifully and abundantly in a few days.

The endosperm of seed is the storehouse of carbohydrates, protein and oil. When the seed germinates, these become predigested amino acids and natural sugars upon which the plant embryo feeds to grow. This life force we eat is filled with energy which is capable of generating cells of the body and supplying us with new vigor and life. For this reason, sprouts can retain the aging process. Sprouts contain goodly amounts of male and female hormones, as well, in their most assimilable form. Research shows that sprouts are among the highest food in vitamins. They are not only a low cost food but are also tasty and easy to grow. Children and the elderly can make sprouting a profitable hobby. All of us can profit from the boost to health they provide and reduce costs in food.

Finally, consider the tremendous potential of sprouts as a survival food. Sprouts alone can sustain and adequately nourish life and growth. If enough seeds are stored and kept dry, millions could be fed in the event of a catastrophe!

Sprouted Grains and Seeds Save $$

It is possible today, even with inflation running between twelve and fourteen percent per year, to save money on, and extend your monies budgeted for your food purchases by learning all about sprouts. There is no other food obtainable that is such a perfect food. Sprouts mixed together with a few other raw vegetables with your favorite salad dressing gives the salad not only more in the way of nutritional value, but taste as well. Our favorite salad is a mixture of alfalfa, mung beans, Alaskan peas, and generous amounts of fresh lettuce, tomatoes, cucumbers, carrots, radishes, and green onions tossed gently together. The final touch for a gourmet's delight is a dressing made with soybean oil and apple cider vinegar mixed with some very special herbs and spices.

Seeds and grains that can be used for sprouting should be a basic part of your food storage program. Because they are so economical, most everyone can afford to store them. Then too, sprouts may be used as a vegetable, on sandwiches, in soups or stews, in breads, cookies, cakes, pancakes and casseroles.

The cost of seeds vary depending upon the amount of and type of seeds purchased. However, my personal research has revealed these interesting facts. One teaspoon of alfalfa seeds weigh 2.33 grams, three teaspoons of alfalfa seeds weigh one ounce or ten grams. Twenty teaspoons of alfalfa seeds weigh four ounces. Therefore, eighty teaspoons of alfalfa seeds weigh one pound and would yield twelve gallons of sprouts. In most health food stores today, the average cost of alfalfa seeds per pound is $2.79, and since one teaspoon of seeds is enough to yield one quart of sprouts, the cost per quart of sprouts is further cut to 29 cents. Thus, giving a crop of fresh vegetables full of all the vitamins and nutrients to build, repair, and maintain a healthy body at a cost that makes them available to everyone.

How to Sprout

Commercially manufactured sprouters may be purchased from local retail health food stores. For the economy minded, however, a quart jar, rubber band or jar ring, and a clean piece of nylon stocking will do. We have several that were constructed by manufacturers, but our favorite method of growing sprouts is the jar method. We simply use a few different size jars: a quart jar for mung beans and wheat; a gallon jar for alfalfa, etc.

In order to yield a crop of excellent sprouts you must first sort through the seeds, beans, and grains you are going to use, picking out all the damaged and broken ones before you start your sprouting process. Now you are ready to sprout.

How to Sprout Wheat

Commercially manufactured sprouters may be purchased from local retailers. However, for the economy minded, a quart jar, rubber band or jar ring, and a clean piece of nylon stocking will do.

1. Add one-half cup wheat to a quart jar. Cover the grain with warm water and soak overnight.
2. Next morning, cover the jar with a rubber band or jar ring. Pour water off the grain through nylon and rinse several times with warm water (never cold), shaking gently until all water is gone.
3. Give the jar a shake and roll to make sure the grain clings to the sides of the jar. Prop at 45 degree angle for drainage (grain will spoil if there is too much water remaining in the jar) on a shelf or drain board.
4. Gently rinse the sprouts with warm water several times a day. Never allow sprouts to become too wet or too dry.

5. In two or three days wheat sprouts will be approximately the length of the seeds. They are ready to eat or refrigerate. After experimenting a few times you will become an expert on sprouting.

Directions For Alfalfa Sprouts

In sprouting another fact to remember is that the seeds are untreated. Manufacturers have not had the opportunity to pretreat these products with their unhealthy preservatives.

1. For a 1-quart sprout jar use one rounded tablespoon of alfalfa seeds. For a 2-quart sprout jar use 2 rounded tablespoons of alfalfa seeds. For a gallon jar use ¼ cup of alfalfa seeds.

2. Place the seeds in the jar and cover with water adding a strainer top, leaving off the solid lid for storing sprouts in the refrigerator later.

3. Let soak overnight with water to cover over the top by about one half to one inch.

4. The following morning pour off all the water through the strainer top into a cup, and rinse the seeds thoroughly with warm tap water. Gently shake the excess water off the seeds. Turn the sprouter jar in a circular motion, allowing the soaked seeds to cling to the sides of the sprouter jar and lay the jar on one side with the top pointed downward. Tilt or prop it at a 45 degree angle.

5. Rinse the seeds twice daily with warm tap water through the strainer top, by filling the jar about one third full of water. Swirl it around, then pour off all excess water. Again shake gently, swirl seeds around the jar, and lay the jar on its side in propped position.

6. Keep the seeds moist but not wet. Do not use artificially softened water.

The strainer top is left on throughout the sprouting process, providing plenty of ventilation. It is not necessary to cover the sprout jar at any time during the sprouting process. Continue the rinsing morning and evening for about five days, at which time depending on (1) the inside temperature of your home and (2) the weather outside, tiny green leaves will appear. At this point, the more light they are exposed to, the greener and more lush the alfalfa sprouts will be. When the little green leaves are fully open on the alfalfa sprouts they are at the peak of their value and ready to use.

How to Wash and Separate Alfalfa Sprouts

After the fifth day wash the sprouts in a collander or, better still, place your sprouts in a bowl of water. Separate them and refill the sprout jar by dropping them lightly into the jar a few at a time so they do not pack. Replace the strainer top, drain off excess water and place the jar on its side as before. By morning you will find the sprouts have filled the jar completely. They are now ready to be eaten, or they can be stored in the refrigerator for one week.

Start another batch right away in another jar, or place the sprouts in another container. Rinse your jar well, and start over again. Always keep sprouts going for daily use. Larger seeds such as soybeans, mung beans, wheat and others will require larger amounts of seeds, depending on the quantity desired.

Recommended Seeds For Your First Sprouting Experience

We suggest that your first crops be alfalfa, mung or aduki beans, and wheat. Since soybeans are difficult to sprout and those older than one year may not sprout at all, it is not advisable to begin with these, or any of the legume family when first learning to sprout. If in your enthusiasm you sprout too large a crop of sprouts, be aware that alfalfa, lentils, garbanzos, and wheat usually are still edible for a week or so. Aduki and mung beans lose their crispness after about three to five days and rye sprouts should be eaten within two to three days after sprouting.

It is advisable to sprout in quantities that will be eaten within three to four days and get into the habit of having a sprout garden in various stages for a continuous fresh supply—some soaking, some germinating and some in the refrigerator. Remember, sprouting increases the volume of the seeds. Twenty pounds of grain or seeds will yield 300-400 pounds of live food.

It is further suggested that a supply of seeds and grains for sprouting be included in your food storage program. In making your purchases the larger the quantity you buy the less the cost per pound.

Amount of Seeds to Store for One Adult for One Year

Type of Seed	*Amount*
Seeds	
Alfalfa	8 lbs.
Chia	8 lbs.
Flax	8 lbs.
Pumpkin	8 lbs.
Radish	8 lbs.
Sesame	8 lbs.
Sunflower	8 lbs.
Beans	
Adzuki	8 lbs.
Black	8 lbs.
Lima	8 lbs.
Mung	8 lbs.
Pinto	20 lbs.
Red	20 lbs.
Soy	20 lbs.
Grains	
Millet	8 lbs.
Oats	8 lbs.
Rice	8 lbs.
Rye	12 lbs.
Wheat	30 lbs.
Peas	
Alaskan	12 lbs.
Black-eyed	12 lbs.

Recipes Using Sprouts

Sprouts With Hotcakes

Make your own favorite hotcake batter. Pour hotcakes out on griddle. Sprinkle a few chopped bean sprouts over them before turning.

Tossed Green and Sprout Salad

6 leaves Romain lettuce
1 green onion, sliced thinly
1 carrot, shredded
¼ cup parsley, chopped
Roquefort cheese dressing

few sprigs watercress
1 cup alfalfa sprouts
¼ cup chicory, chopped
1 cup mung bean sprouts

Tear leaves gently into a salad bowl well rubbed with garlic. Add other ingredients, then pour dressing over. Toss lightly together and serve immediately. Never add salt of any flavor to salad until after it has been served. Salt draws the water out of vegetables, making the salad soggy.

Spinach Salad

1 lb. fresh spinach
2 tbsp. lemon juice
½ tsp. salt
4 green onions and tops sliced
coarsely ground black pepper
1 coarsely chopped hard-cooked egg

5 slices bacon, diced
1 tsp. sugar
½ cup bean sprouts

Wash spinach, discarding stems. Pat dry on paper towels, then tear in bite size pieces into a bowl. Add onions and sprinkle with pepper. Chill. At serving time, slowly fry bacon bits in a deep chafing dish or electric skillet until crisp. Add vinegar, lemon juice, sugar and salt. Add spinach, then toss just till leaves are coated and wilted slightly. Sprinkle with egg. Serves 6.

Sprouted Whole Wheat Bread

Into a large mixing bowl pour 1 cup lukewarm water. Add 2 tablespoons dry yeast. Let dissolve.

Add: 2 cups warm water, 2 tbsp. salt, ¼ cup honey and 3 tbsp. oil or margarine.

Stir in: 3½ cups unbleached white flour

Beat dough till elastic. Let this sponge rise. Keep temperature around 80 degrees. To raised sponge add 2 cups wheat sprouts, whole or ground in meat grinder. Work in about 2 cups whole wheat flour. Knead until dough is smooth and elastic. Place in oiled bowl. Cover and let rise in warm place until doubled in bulk. Knead lightly, shape into loaves. Place in greased loaf pans. Let rise until doubled. Bake at 375 degrees for 25 minutes, or 300 degrees for 35 minutes.

Graham Muffins

Mix:

2 eggs, beaten	1½ cup sour milk
3 tbsp. melted butter	

Sift together and add:

¼ cup sugar	½ tsp. salt
1 tsp. soda	1 tsp. baking powder
1 cup unbleached white flour	
1½ cup graham flour or whole wheat	

Stir until well blended, then add ¼ to ½ cup chopped sprouts (your favorite). Bake at 425° for 15 to 20 minutes. Makes 20 muffins.

Alfalfa Sprout Dip

1 pint dairy sour cream	1 tbsp. beef soup base
2 tbsp. minced instant onion	¼ to ½ cup chopped alfalfa

Mix together and serve

Try sprouts:

On a peanut butter and jelly sandwich;
with honey and raisins for a treat;
in jello for a salad delight;
in soup, stews, casseroles, and main dishes;
in mashed potatoes;

in gravy;
in stuffing;
on top of hors d'oeuvers;
in spaghetti sauce;
in meat loaf;
in cooked or dry cereal;
in just about anything you want to use them in.

Sprouted Wheat Balls

2 cups sprouted wheat   2 cups bread crumbs
1 cup almonds, walnuts or pecans 1 tsp. salt
1 large onion   2 tbsp. oil
1 cup milk

Put sprouts, almonds, and onions through the small blade of a meat grinder. Add crumbs, salt, oil. Stir in milk. Make into balls. Bake in oven on a greased cookie sheet or frying pan until golden brown. Serve with gravy. Top with parsley.

Vegetable Sprout Casserole

½ cup diced carrots or pimento
1 finely chopped onion or leek
1½ cup fresh or frozen peas
1 to 1½ cup mung bean sprouts
2 tbsp. chopped parsley
½ to 1 cup shredded cheese
½ cup buttered bread crumbs
paprika

Cook carrots and onions in a small amount of water. After 10 minutes add peas. When almost tender, add sprouts and parsley. Continue cooking 5 minutes more. Fold vegetables together with cream sauce (see below). Place in a greased casserole dish. Top with shredded cheese and bread crumbs. Sprinkle with paprika. Bake uncovered at 350 degrees for 20 to 30 minutes.

Cream Sauce

Melt over low heat, 2 tbsp. butter. Add 1½ tbsp. flour. Blend over low heat 3 to 5 minutes. Stir in slowly 2 cups milk.

Add 2 cloves and 1 bay leaf. Cook and stir over low heat until thick. Remove cloves and bay leaf.

Bean Sprout Salad

1 head Romain lettuce	1 cucumber
3 tomatoes	2 cups bean sprouts
Radishes and olives to garnish	Sour cream dressing

Place Romain leaves on salad plates. Place a layer of bean sprouts on these. Slice alternate layers of cucumber and tomato over them, tapering up to a peak the last layer being cucumber. Garnish with ripe olives and radishes. Serve with dressing.

Chapter Thirty-one

How to Wash
on a Rub Board

We are experienced in this activity, although it has been many years since we have actually applied the theory. We are going to attempt to write about it.

Reading instructions is not enough; you will have to learn by doing. However, we are going to give a few simple instructions to help you learn, should the need arise.

The materials you will need are:

3 large wash tubs
1 large metal rub board
1 bar laundry soap
clothes pins and clothes pin bag

hot and cold water
laundry hamper
laundry basket

1. Heat the water in one of the tubs over a hot fire.

2. Set the other two tubs up on blocks or a tree stump side by side about fifteen feet away from the fire.

3. Make certain all tubs are secure.

4. Fill one tub with boiling water, adding enough cold water to make it tolerable for your hands.

5. Add a few white clothes to the wash water.

6. Put the rub board in the tub and rub the surface with a bar of soap.

7. Take a piece of laundry out of the water, lay it the length of and on top of the wash board. Rub soap on material.

8. With the edge of the material held in your hand between thumb and fingers, begin to rub up and down the board with the heel of your hand, gathering and pulling the material toward you.

9. Push the material down in the water and begin from the beginning.

10. Scrub each garment vigorously four to eight times.

11. Dip into water, rinse, wring out water, put in next tub, filled with warm rinse water.

12. Rinse in second water, wring dry, hang on clothes line.

Sound complicated? Not really, after a few blisters and a sore back you will fast become an expert.

For best results, boil the clothes in boiling water for about one hour, stirring occasionally. This will loosen the soil and make scrubbing on the rub board much easier.

Chapter Thirty-two

How to Build a Small Animal Trap

The real beauty of this particular trap is that it may be constructed either with or without nails. It is compact, easily contructed, and it does work.

Another important factor to remember is that the trap is mobile. If one place is not suitable, you may pick it up and move it to another place.

You may build this trap any size you wish, either 3, 4, or 5 feet square. Use ¾" x 2" boards or split shakes, and stack them in a pyramid (see diagram), making each board two inches shorter than the succeeding one. Leave ½" to 1" of space between the boards and nail each corner. If nails are not available, cut a small green branch about as large around as your index finger, and tie the branch to the bottom board on the left side, across the top and down to the bottom board on the right side, binding all the boards together in a tight pyramid.

Selecting Proper Sites

Rabbits—Locate feeding grounds, pick a secluded area near an old road or edge of field.

Pheasants—Locate feeding area—set near fields or edge of woods.

Quail—Locate roosting places, set trap nearby.

How to Set the Trap

Clear the ground on the spot you are going to set the trap and make the surface as smooth as possible. Build the trap and prop it up (see diagram), set the triggers. Bait the trap with an ear of corn, bread crumbs, or whatever you may have, both under the trap and about one or two feet around and away from the front of the trap. Make sure most of the bait is under the trap. You may leave and come back in a few hours when trapped small animals cannot get out.

Note: If quail are trapped in this manner, make sure to pick up any and all loose feathers, otherwise other quail will not come near the trap again.

TRAP: FOR SMALL ANIMALS OR BIRDS

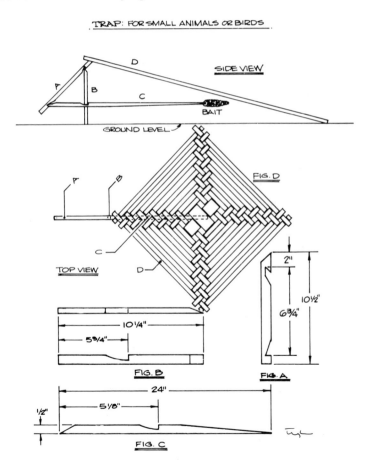

Chapter Thirty-three

Storage Utensils

In this chapter, as in some of the previous ones, the utensils for a Home Storage and Production Program depend entirely upon the individual family needs and financial resources. The items listed in this chapter are to be used as a guide to enable everyone to have as complete a year's supply as their circumstances will allow.

1. Sewage Disposal: One covered metal container (small enough to be used as a toilet).
2. One large 20-gallon garbage can with a tight fitting lid. Secure the lid to the can with a piece of rope to prevent loss. Line the can with a large plastic bag to hold the waste until it can be disposed of. If human waste is buried, make sure to bury it at least 18 to 24 inches deep.
3. At least two lanterns, either Coleman or kerosene, extra wicks, mantles, and extra globes.
4. Flashlight, extra batteries, and bulbs
5. Water purification tablets
6. Camp stove or some other method for cooking
7. Scrubbing brush, lots of clean rags
8. Case of stick matches (keep dry)
9. Plastic garbage bags
10. Extra newspapers (clean)
11. Broom
12. Transistor radio, extra batteries

13. Case of toilet tissue, or more
14. Vitamins
15. Two large wash tubs
16. Clothes pins
17. Wire or rope for clothesline
18. Rub board
19. Clock (manual)
20. Dish pan (metal)
21. Wash pan (small wash hands)
22. Safety pins
23. Manually operated grain mill
24. Flat irons

Chapter Thirty-four

Handy Hints

1. Leavening Agents
   1 whole egg equals ½ tsp. baking powder
   1 egg white equals ½ tsp. baking powder
   ½ tsp. soda equals 2 tsp. baking powder
   ¼ tsp. soda and ½ tsp. cream tartar equals 1 tsp. baking powder

2. For an emergency water supply, fill empty canning jars with water, store on pantry shelf.

3. Oatmeal water can be used for treating poison oak or poison ivy. Cook ½ cup oats in 1 quart water. Bathe infected parts, pat dry.

4. For athlete's foot, rub a clove of pure garlic on the infected area.

5. Use baking soda as:
   a. toothpaste,
   b. deodorant,
   c. a pot scrubber. Use full strength on a damp cloth
   d. fire extinguisher. Use full strength at the base of flames in grease and electric fires.
   e. mouthwash. Dissolve 1 tsp. baking soda in ½ glass water.

f. body deodorant. Mix 2 tsp. baking soda, 2 tsp. petroleum jelly and 2 tsp. talcum powder. Heat in double boiler over low heat and stir until a smooth cream forms. Put cream in a small container with a tight lid and use as you would a regular cream deodorant.

6. For candles that do not fit tightly in their holders, try wrapping a rubber band around the bottom several times.

7. Soak new brooms in strong hot salt water before using. This toughens the bristles and makes the broom last longer.

8. Suggested Uses For Salt:
   a. ½ tsp. in glass warm water for headache and indigestion.
   b. 1 tsp. in quart warm water for enema, cleanser, healer and natural bowel movement.
   c. 1 tsp. in glass of warm water for laxative.
   d. 1 tsp. in glass warm water for gargle.
   e. sprinkle on open cuts, it is a natural healer.

9. Suggested Uses for Vinegar;
   a. 1 tsp. of vinegar in a pint of furniture polish will add luster to your furniture.
   b. 1 tsp. vinegar added to the rinse water will help nylon stockings retain their elasticity.
   c. Soaking clothes in warm vinegar removes perspiration stains.
   d. 1 tsp. vinegar in frying oil will prevent the food from absorbing so much oil.
   e. When boiling potatoes, add a tsp. of vinegar to the water to keep the potatoes from turning dark.
   f. When poaching eggs, add a tsp. of vinegar to the water to keep the egg whites from spreading.
   g. Add 1 tsp. vinegar to the water when boiling rice to keep the grains whole.
   h. A tbsp. of vinegar added to the water in which beef is boiled will make the meat tender.
   i. To cause cream or milk to sour, add one tbsp. of vinegar per cup.

k. Boiling cracked eggs in water with a little vinegar will keep the egg whites from running out of shells.

l. Harboiled eggs are easier to peel if a little vinegar is added to water while boiling.

m. To prevent food from sticking to a new fry pan, boil a little vinegar in it prior to use.

n. A little vinegar rubbed on sunburn will take away the sting.

Part 10

Survival
Library

Chapter Thirty-five

Other Sources of Information

Food Storage

Anderson, Aruthur W., *Bee Prepared With Honey*
    Published by Horizon Publishers, Bountiful, Utah 1975
Batchelor, Walter D., *Gateway To Survival Is Storage*
    Published Mesa, Arizona 1968
Briscoe, Alan K., *Timely Tips On Quantity Food Buying*
    Published by Horizon Publishers, Bountiful, Utah 1974
Briscoe, Alan K., *Your Guide To Home Storage*
    Published by Horizon Publishers, Bountiful, Utah 1974
Dickey, Esther, *Passport To Survival*
    Published by Bookcraft, Inc., Salt Lake City, Utah 1969
Dienstbier, Hendricks, *Natural Foods Storage Bible*
    Published by Horizon Publishers, Bountiful, Utah 1976
Egan, Meritt H.N.D., *Home Storage*
    Published by Welfare Department, The Church of Jesus
    Christ of Latter-day Saints, Salt Lake City, Utah 1959
FAO—Who, Energy and Protein Requirement, in press 1972
Hertzberg, R. Vaughn B., and Green, J., *Putting Food By*
    Published by The Steven Green Press 1973
Holley, Beverly B., *Pantry Partner*
    Published by Horizon Publishers, Bountiful, Utah 1974
Mehew, Randall K., *Basic Home Storage Guide*
    Published by Horizon Publishers, Bountiful, Utah 1977
Nelson, Louise E., *Project Readiness*
    Published by Horizon Publishers, Bountiful, Utah 1974

Recommended Dietary Allowances, Food and Nutrition Board, Published 1964, 7th edition, Washington, D.C. National Research Council, National Academy of Sciences, 1968

Salsbury, Barbara G., *Just In Case*
   Published by Bookcraft Inc., Salt Lake City, Utah 1975

Sam Andy Foods, *Food Storage Guide And Cookbook*
   Published by United Commodities International, Colton, California 1969

Zabriskie, Bob R., *Family Storage Plan*
   Published by Bookcraft, Inc., Salt Lake City, Utah 1966

Food Preparation

Ashdown, Greta, *Fruit Season*
   Published by Ashdown House, Bountiful Utah

Bills, Jay & Shirley, *Home Food Dehydrating*
   Published by Horizon Publishers, Bountiful, Utah 1973

Briscoe, Alan K., *Soybean Granule Recipes*
   Published by Horizon Publishers, Bountiful, Utah 1974

Composition of Foods—Raw, Process, Prepared, U.S. Dept. of Agriculture Handbook No. 8, Washington, D.C., Government Printing Office 1963

Davis, Gary, *Kitchen Garden Sprouts And Recipe Book*
   Published by Kitchen Garden, Salt Lake City, Utah, 1972

Densley, Barbara, *ABC's of Home Food Dehydration*
   Published by Horizon Publishers, Bountiful, Utah, 1975

El Molino Mills *El Molino Best Recipes*
   Published by John M. McCoy Printers, Inc., Alhambra, California 1972

Ethington, Evelyn C., *Creative Wheat Cookery*
   Published by Horizon Publishers, Bountiful, Utah 1975

Flack, Dora D., *Dry & Save*
   Published by Bookcraft Inc., Salt Lake City, Utah 1976

Flack, Dora D., *Fun With Fruit Preservation*
   Published by Horizon Publishers, Bountiful, Utah 1973

Jardine, Winifred C., *Famous Mormon Recipes*
   Published by Liddle Enterprises, Inc., Salt Lake City, Utah 1972

Jones, Dorothea Van Gunday, *The Soybean Cookbook*
   Published by Arco Publishing Company, Inc., New York, New York, 1973

Kloss, Jethro, *Back To Eden*
   Published by Lifeline Books, Riverside, California 1973

Laughlin, Ruth, *Natural Sweets And Treats*
   Published by Bookcraft Inc., Salt Lake City, Utah 1973
Larimore, Bertha B., *Sprouting For All Seasons*
   Published by Horizon Publishers, Bountiful, Utah 1975
Moulton, Le Arta, *The Gluten Book*
   Published by The Gluten Co. Inc., Provo, Utah 1974
Ortho Book Series, *12 Months Harvest*
   Published by Ortho Book Division, San Francisco, Calif.,
   1975
Perma Pak, *Culinary Capers*
   Published by Perma Pak Inc., Salt Lake City, Utah 1975
Reynolds, Brumford Scott, *How To Survive With Sprouting*
   Published by Hawkes Publishing Inc., Salt Lake City, Utah
   1970
Richards, Hazel, *Make A Treat With Wheat*
   Published by Hawkes Publishing Inc., Salt Lake City, Utah
   1968
Rosenvall, V.; Miller, M.; Flack, D., *Wheat For Man*
   Published by Bookcraft, Inc., Salt Lake City, Utah 1966
Salsbury, Barbara G., *Just Add Water*
   Published by Horizon Publishers, Bountiful, Utah 1972
Salsbury, Barbara G., *Tasty Imitations*
   Published by Horizon Publishers, Bountiful, Utah 1973
Stephensen, Ruth, *Mix 'N Moisten Meals*
   Published by Bookcraft, Inc., Salt Lake City, Utah 1974
Sudweeks, Deanna Smith, *Kitchen Magic*
   Published by Kitchen Magic, Pleasant Grove, Utah 1975
United States Department of Agriculture *Home And Garden
   Bulletin No. 72,* Published Washington, D.C. 1970

Miscellaneous Information

Allen, G. and Muller, A., *Sprouts How to Grow and Eat Them*
   Published Felton, California 1973
Angier, Bradford, *Feasting Free On Wild Edibles*
Angier, Bradford, *Field Guide To Edible Wild Plants*
Angier, Bradford, *Survival With Style—In Trouble Or In Fun*
   Published by Stackpole Books, Harrisburg, Penn. 1972
Barker, Harriett, *The One Burner Gourmet*
   Published by Greatlakes Living Press, Matteson, Ill. 1975
Bowers, Warner & Lucile, *Common Sense Organic Gardening*
   Published by Stackpole Books, Harrisburg, Penn. 1974

Churchill, James E., *Homesteaders Homebook, The*
   Published by Stackpole Books, Harrisburg, Penn. 1974
Home Family Medical Emergencies
Jenkins, Jack and Bingham, Larry *The Equi-Flo System Of Dehydration* Published Marysville, Washington
Mac Maniman, Gen *Dry It You'll Like It*
   Published by Mac Maniman Inc., Fall City, Washington 1974
Mittleider, J.R., *More Food From Your Garden*
   Published by Woodbridge Press, Santa Barbara, Calif. 1975
New Essential First Aid
Newquist, Jerrald L., *Prophets, Principles And National Survival* Published by Publishers Press, Salt Lake City, Utah 1964
Page, Roland, *How To Be Prepared For Any Crisis*
   Published by Hawkes Publishing Inc., Salt Lake City, Utah 1974
Rasmussen, Dean L., *How To Live Through A Famine*
   Published by Horizon Publishers, Bountiful, Utah 1976
Ridley, Clifford, *How To Grow Your Own Groceries For $100 A Year* Published by Hawkes Publishing Inc., Salt Lake Utah 1974
Ruff, Howard J., *Famine And Survival In America*
   Published by Target Publishing, Alamo, California 1974
Stevsen, James T., *Making The Best Of Basics*
   Published by Peton Corporation, Salt Lake City, Utah 1976
U.S. Department of Defense *Family Guide Emergency Health Care* Published by U.S. Government Printing Office 1964
Wagginton, Eliot *The Foxfire Book, Foxfire Two,* and *Foxfire Three,* Published by Anchor Press, Garden City, N.Y. 1969

Index